second banana
dottie lamm

Johnson Books: Boulder

First Printing September 1983
Second Printing November 1983

ISBN 0-933472-79-X

LCCN: 83-082217

Cover Photograph and Design: Joseph Daniel

Printed in the United States of America by

Johnson Publishing Company
1880 South 57th Court
Boulder, Colorado 80302

To Dick—
    Husband
    Lover
    Father
    Friend
    And absolutely *Top* Banana

In Loving Memory of Four Friends
who died young

Donna Arnold Haywood
Diane Collins Nickerson
Jessica Martinez Luna
Linda Geroski Avery

Contents

Acknowledgments

I am deeply indebted to the following people, without whose inspiration these columns and this book might not have been written: my father, the late John K. Vennard, who taught me that when something needed writing to write it; my mother, Dorothy Walton Vennard, for being her ever-growing, ever-loving, and supportive self; my husband, Dick Lamm, for pushing me to get this project done and for suggesting the title; my in-laws, Arnold and Mary Lamm, for their many insights on family issues; my children, Scott and Heather Lamm, for contributing more than they know—and perhaps more than they wanted to; my sister, Jane Vennard, my alter-ego and friend of 40 years; my women's support group, for a dozen years of "being there," especially when other relationships seemed dry, sparse, and fragile.

My deep appreciation also goes to my Palo Alto High School English teacher, Craig Vittetoe, for inspiring me to think as well as write; to Patsy Cox and Judy Bucher for launching my writing career by publishing my campaign journal in *The Colorado Woman Digest*; to Joan White of the *Denver Post* for being mentor, editor, and friend; to Burdette Knous for her friendship, her typing, and her suggestions for column ideas; to the Editorial Board and staff at the *Denver Post* for their constructive guidance; to Sandra Dallas Atchison for directing me to Johnson Books; to my social work instructors and supervisors who taught me to "listen with the third ear;" to the Colorado Executive Residence staff, the mansion security detail, and the State Historical Society tourguides who, by doing what they do well, allow me to do what I do well; to the photographers and to the people named and unnamed who knowingly and unknowingly provided the material for this book.

Special tribute is also paid to my "informal" support group—those people of like mind who are friends and soulmates, even when not physically present: Phil and Susan Hammer of San Jose, California; Dick and Sigrid Freese of Denver, Colorado; Tom and Lynette Richardson of Aspen, Colorado; Tom and Peggy Lamm of Boulder, Colorado; Terry and Nancy Lamm of Bernilillo, New Mexico; Sue Ward Damour of Denver; Barbara Lamm of Boulder; and Ann DeBusk of Stanford, California.

My respectful appreciation also goes to former First Lady Betty Ford, whose support, guidance, and inspiration helped me through my recovery from breast cancer.

Although there are literary references in this collection, most of the material was provided by everyday people and everyday life. I am indebted to all those who helped me see, sift, and evaluate the human experience.

Introduction

In 1976, the year of the nation's bicentennial and Colorado's centennial, an exhibit on western women called "Hidden Faces" toured the state. Its sketches and photographs celebrated the women behind the scenes—the women who were the unsung homemakers, ranch hands, school teachers, and laborers in the settling of the West.

The exhibit was historical, but the year 1976 had its own "hidden faces." That year, a small but intense group of women called the League of Housewives escalated a drive to remove Colorado's Equal Rights Amendment from the state constitution. Another small, but equally determined, group of feminists led by the National Organization for Women vowed to preserve the ERA at all costs. From opposite poles, LOH and NOW challenged each other. In the middle were the "hidden faces," the seemingly voiceless silent majority: the voters. When Amendment No. 8, the Repeal of the ERA, faced them on the November ballot, which way would they go?

Just when it appeared the voters might be irretrievably polarized, a group emerged which was to spearhead the pro-Equal Rights Amendment forces. The group, which became known as Homemakers for ERA, evolved into a voice both soft and strong; a voice with which those "hidden faces" behind the city, suburban, and rural doors might identify.

I accompanied those feminist homemakers as they diligently walked from door to door, talking confidently of equality for women and parity for homemakers, bearing testimony to the fact that one needn't be a career woman to be a feminist. Most of the women they approached opened their doors, their minds, and their hearts. In turn, they communicated their enthusiasm for the ERA to the men with whom they resided. On election day, the Colorado ERA was retained by a two-to-one margin.

After the election I began to think about how the voice of these moderate feminist homemakers could be sustained. How could it be translated to other homemakers and to career women who were feminist by inclination, but either didn't know it or wouldn't admit it, women not with hidden faces, but perhaps with hidden thoughts? The seed of an idea was growing. Could I be a voice for the woman who says, "I believe in equal pay, but I'm not sure I'm a feminist"; or, "I'm not a 'woman's libber,' but . . . I wish my husband would help a little more with the kids"?

Could I help these women express themselves and see that being family-centered and being feminist were not incompatible or mutually exclusive? Why not? I had been both a career woman and a homemaker, a part-time social worker and a full-time mother. As First Lady I had a unique platform from which to speak of these experiences and others. In 1978, I approached *The Denver Post* with my idea and was encouraged to try it.

Since February of 1979 I have been meeting a deadline for my *Post* column, which first appeared weekly and now appears twice a week in the *Living* and *Contemporary* sections. I believe that my original goal of speaking to the untapped and unrecognized feminist in a language she could understand has worked. I have received hundreds of letters validating that success. But my column has become something else, something to which men as well as women have responded.

As I have selected, edited, and rearranged the 80 columns chosen for this book (out of more than 200 published), I have discovered an unexpected pattern and seen a new gestalt emerge. Yes, this book is about feminism. But feminism is only one part of a bigger whole. What this book is really about is relationships.

It is about the relationship of a wife to a publicly acclaimed or highly visible and highly successful husband; hence the title *Second Banana*.

It is about the relationship of women to men, spouse to

spouse, women to women, and sometimes men to men. It is about the relationship of child to parent, friend to friend, employee to boss, the individual to the society in which he or she lives.

It is about the relationship not only between people, but the relationship of each person's parts to his or her whole. It explores not only personalities, but what the late psychoanalyst Roberto Assagioli calls the "sub-personalities" of individuals. It does not solve relationship problems or give pat answers, but explores what columnist Ellen Goodman has called the on-going "ambivalence of life."

Second Banana is also about the relationship of an individual to his/her God. This fact astounded me as I realized it, for until my bout with breast cancer in 1981, I saw the spiritual and religious areas as outside the perimeters of my expertise. Yet, as Rabbi Harold Kushner writes in *When Bad Things Happen to Good People*, "Human beings are God's language." As a trained psychiatric social worker, I know that human beings *are* within the perimeters of my expertise.

More than 60 years ago, columnist Walter Lippmann wrote: "We are unsettled to the very roots of our being. There isn't a human relation, whether of parent to child, husband and wife, worker and employer, that doesn't move in a strange situation. We are not used to a complicated civilization: we don't know how to behave when personal conduct and external authority have disappeared. There are no precedents to guide us, no wisdom that wasn't made for a simpler age. We have changed our environment more quickly than we know how to change ourselves."

His words seem even truer today. If these columns are somewhat unsettling, it's because the times are unsettling and this author often is unsettled.

Since I began writing in 1979, readers have encouraged me to put my columns in book form. In 1982, while recovering from breast cancer, I felt moved to take their advice.

Newspaper columns are like so much buckshot from a shotgun. They hit. They miss. They are absorbed. They are ignored. They are attached to the white refrigerator door with a red ladybug magnet. They are used to wrap the fishbones that can't go into the disposal. Suddenly, I wanted to preserve some of my columns in a comprehensive, tangible form, something that might outlast me.

The sections of this book are arranged topically rather than chronologically. Often they overlap. Like the climb up a mountain of shale, the progression of my ideas sometimes takes two steps forward, only to slide back one. One column may contradict another immediately preceding, because occasionally I find myself agreeing with Supreme Court Justice Felix Frankfurter when he said, "It does not appear to appear to me now, as it appeared to appear to me then."

The first and last sections of this book differ somewhat from the rest: the first is composed, not of *Post* columns, but of the diary I kept during my husband's first campaign for the Governorship. It was originally published in the *Colorado Woman Digest*. The last section is composed of poetry, written during my convalescence from surgery and my thirteen month chemotherapy period. The collection includes a poem written to me by my husband during my hospitalization.

In my first column in 1979, I wrote that I had always dreamed of a professional arena in which I could put my political, social-work, homemaker, and motherhood experience to work simultaneously. This book is that "arena." But that doesn't mean it should be read all at once. Read it at random. Consider it a friend you can cultivate, abandon, and return to.

I: The Beginning

For all those spouses who are so much a part of a team they sometimes forget who they are—

My complaints of being "put upon" are because I don't know where to put myself.

Ethel Seldin-Schwartz

JOURNAL: An Examination of the Feminist Dilemma

My husband became governor of Colorado in 1974. As we campaigned, won, and moved from a modest home with a part-time babysitter to a 25-room mansion with a staff of seven and security guards around the clock, I began to record my thoughts and have continued to do so. The dilemmas of a feminist-spouse of a politician may be similar to those of a feminist-spouse of a non-politician, only more magnified.

I originally wrote only for the clarification of my own thoughts and feelings, but I now find myself wanting to share. It occurs to me that many political wives express their feelings and conflicts only when their husbands are out of office—with the obvious benefits and safety of hindsight. I would like to share while the insights are fresh and the adjustment still not complete. Only in the present tense can my feminist experience have its greatest potential of relating to someone else's.

Fall 1973: The Race Begins

I am happy, now that we are truly involved in a joint venture—his campaign—at how important I have become.

Yet, I am furious! Wasn't my life important before? And weren't our children a joint venture? Would we be so close *if it were I who was running*?

I am finding the ordinary more and more difficult—the cooking, the cleaning, the shopping. I'm wanting to do these things all the more creatively when I hardly have time to do them at all. My tastes have outpaced my abilities, and I have no time to develop them. Yesterday I let everything go and baked bread, just to keep in touch; suddenly I needed to be restored by the same recipe which had consoled me when my father died. A part of me seems to be dying, as I father, mother, organize, and campaign—and at such a pace! I am successful, but there is *no emotional space for me*.

* * *

Our campaign includes an 800-mile walk the length of the state. I like the way he laughs deep about nothing when he has just come home from walking. Absences are hell on the family; our little boy spins out of control or walks in solemn circles. We all feel desolate and deserted. Yet, he is so exhilarated when he returns, I wish that he would walk some more.

* * *

There is now a momentum growing that is as engulfing as falling in love or finding a dream. There are no greater or lesser jobs, no stereotyping of duties, as I had heretofore experienced in marriage. We each do what needs to be done. If I'm not here and the children need to be fed, he feeds them; if he's not here and a speech needs to be given, I give it. Everything is important, the cost of each sacrifice unweighed and automatically accepted. We lose ourselves to the process. A mission is to be accomplished. I imagine us homesteading or setting out to conquer the West in a covered wagon.

* * *

Spring 1974: Confrontations and Fears

Daily we are forced to come to grips with ourselves and with problems which private life often allowed us to avoid. Our opponents in the Democratic Primary are friends and close political colleagues. Although most of us, unconsciously at least, compete with those we love and often admire those with whom we compete, it is difficult to integrate at the conscious level such diametrically opposed feelings and ambitions. (It is far easier to hate the enemy!) Yet, day after day, speech after speech, we have to confront and contain our conflicting feelings in order to walk that delicate balance of promoting one's self without putting down the other.

* * *

Today, I implied to a group of women that I had no personal ambitions of my own and almost believed it! Incredible. Someday I would like to be a highly successful therapist, journalist, or legislator. "B.S." may be a necessary part of political life; if I cannot eliminate it, at least I will be conscious of it when I use it! The biggest danger is in "B.S.-ing" myself!

* * *

Twice in a crowded swimming pool I have caught myself, out of sudden anger, jostling bothersome people. This is a vicious and devious hostility of which I'm ashamed. Loud noises bother me. When I am driving, automobiles approaching me from the intersecting streets at the right make me jump and apply the brakes much as I did after our car accident ten years ago. I dream of vague and impending disaster. I feel propelled into situations for which I am not ready. Are my negative actions and reactions really new, or are the strains of the campaign just keeping me more in touch with them?

* * *

People ask me, "How will it feel to be the governor's wife?"

"It depends on who is governor!" I say with a grin. Inwardly, I fear it won't be my husband.

Fall 1974: Victory

The joy of winning is subdued by numbness and growing awe at the responsibility. I suddenly realize that I can be a powerful influence for women, children, the Equal Rights Amendment, or anything else I choose. I am terrified of the potential for success and for failure. Just yesterday, we were still "running." Today, I feel like running away.

* * *

Friends arrive at the door bearing flowers and gifts. I'm suddenly embarrassed; I feel run down, vulnerable, and inadequate in my worn-out campaign outfit. They are relieved to see that I still look like me. I feel reassured, glowing, and content.

* * *

The children's adjustability is frightening! Because of a threat on the life of a political colleague, uniformed policemen with shotguns are staying in our small living room. By the third night the children's initial amazement at their presence has turned from mild curiosity to total acceptance. Humankind's adaptability may be its own worst enemy. Is humanity capable of psychologically and environmentally adjusting itself right out of freedom or life itself? Will we adjust so well to our new positions that we will not recognize ourselves when we're done?

* * *

The campaign has brought us together like nothing else in eleven years. I am anguished that just as I am free enough to think of him as my best friend, he will be less and less available to me. The number of planning sessions for the new administration multiply by the day. What will it be like after the inauguration?

1975: Post-Election Settling In

Winning has been like having our first baby: we planned, we prepared, we rejoiced in the accomplishment. It is only later that the endlessness of the responsibility and the tedium of detail slowly dawn. The demands are incessant. I have the sinking feeling I will never again have a moment totally alone. The only difference from the depression that follows childbirth is that we are both depressed. When our first child arrived I bore my depression myself. Now we share our misery. We shore each other up to keep going. I wonder if joint depressions, like joint ventures, are only the ones that are the result of male-oriented undertakings.

* * *

I can't stand to be strong, charming, tactful, and careful for one more minute. I like looking beautiful and I like being grubby—I hate always looking "proper." I want to grab my bike and ride in the rain forever, cleansing my mind, washing my body free of its eye infection, backache, and nervous stomach. The weekend is always my breaking point. By then I cannot stand to see one more person; I'm tired of my ineptitudes and mistakes and those of others. Everyone says I'm such a straight talker, such a good example, but I am watching out of the corners of my eyes every minute. One has to go through a procession of help, security, and visitors to even enter or leave the governor's mansion. If I were really natural, would I be a political burden or an asset? I am sick of wrestling with these questions and of keeping everybody's life in order. They can all go hang and keep their own lives in order. How can I be in charge of them; I hardly feel in charge of me.

* * *

I am continually torn between the desire to protect him from the tedious and the tiresome, and the desire to have him struggle with some of the mundane. Those who become involved with only "great" issues gradually become inhuman. I resent it when he cannot deal with detailed and repetitive tasks but still expects such tasks to be performed perfectly by others.

* * *

Women are given trivial tasks, then demeaned and laughed at for being trivial. Does it matter what color tulips come up where as long as they are healthy and long-blooming? All things blend in nature. I can't believe I gave two hours to planning the color of gardens I've not yet seen.

* * *

Male politicians' reactions to the press appear totally irrational. Of course! Once in office, they experience an old infantile rage at "that something" which has a power over their lives, irrespective of their worth, which they have not experienced since they broke ties with their parents. I suffer for them. We women, as we move our identity from parents to husband, live with "that something" daily.

Spring 1976: Revelations

Paid household employees, whom I am finally learning to employ without guilt, are making us an equal team. He and I can now share in the remaining work and the burdens. It used to be, he had the help (me) and I had the burdens! A revelation has hit me! We may not always have paid help, but we will never go back to the old ways! This way of living has shown me the possibility of true teamwork. It neither forces the wife into the traditional support role, nor does it superimpose the stereotyped liberation model, which assumes that each person can pursue his or her "own thing" and never give to the other. We all need support and we all need to give succor. It terrifies me that only by attaining this unique position have I been able to break unquestioned patterns. Hopefully, other women can find their own ways to break their own inhibiting patterns.

* * *

I feel guilty
Since: I love my job
I have power and position
Ways of accomplishing my goals
Love and friendships
That: I am not happy and grateful all the time
I know that it is impossible to be happy
   and grateful
All the time. That is unrealistic
Preposterous. Yet
I feel guilty

* * *

We have different goals for him, the staff and I. They want to direct his growth mainly for the maximum political production. I see his political production as just one aspect of continual growth and change. I will want to live with a human being after all the cheering and booing stops. They will not have to live with him at all.

Summer 1976: Role and Reality

"She's adjusted," said he.
"She's crazy!" said she.
"She *has* adjusted," said he.
"Sanity? The price of adjustment?" asked she.
"Why not?" shrugged he.

* * *

My anger is not at being a woman, but at the smug assumption that if I am a woman, I must. . . . My anger is not at being the governor's wife, but at the smug assumption that if I am the governor's wife, I must. . . . The only real "must" for me is to prioritize my own musts. I am always on the verge of forgetting that.

* * *

I told myself that political life would not change me, yet it has. I cannot say to a Coloradoan, "I like your idea, but I will not get involved—it is not a priority with me." The symbolic role pounds louder in her ears than the person, though I do not wish it to. I must say instead, "I love your idea; I'd love to get involved; I just have too full a schedule this year." Or must I? Do I hide behind stock answers for fear of hurting feelings or losing support? Whatever the reason, the process nags painfully and continually at the edges of my integrity.

* * *

Today I took to lunch a person with whom I was expected (for some unspecified reason) to "cement relations for the future"! How frightening that I could fall into this role! I would rather be phony, conniving, and clawing in pursuit of a specific goal than be innocuously pleasant and superficial to maintain a relationship that means nothing to me. Yet, somehow I at least need to try out what advisors suggest. When my own imperatives are clearer, I will shed such suggestions as I would clothes which don't fit.

Fall 1976: Power–Illusion and Disillusion

The "First Lady" role sometimes feels like it is closing in on me, suffocating me. Yet I relish my role when it can bring validation to a cause in which I am interested. Is this a lust for power or perhaps a "cop-out" in disguise? ("It was the role, not me, that achieved the goal!") A governor's wife, like "wife" and "mother," can claim recognition by another's position, yet take none of the real responsibility. This denial of true responsibility keeps me in a little-girl place, fantasizing about my success but having no way of measuring my real impact.

* * *

I see that the "male" mentality of taking services for granted is not as attributable to being male as it is to power and position.

I am not a male

And yet: I now notice the one time the flowers are forgotten—not the endless days of perfectly prepared tables.

I am not a male

And yet: I come to my children's picnic, full of self-importance, bellowing, "I'm starved!"—not thinking of the work my babysitter and other mothers did to prepare the feast.

I used to fall all over myself thanking people as though I did not feel worthy of their care. Do the entrapments of position make me so "worthy" I can now forget to say "thank you"?

* * *

I thought that I would be different in this position from other politicians; I would lend an ear to all people and problems, then judiciously decide a course of action based on merit. Yet there are only so many people, so many phone calls, and so many problems I can handle a day. My goals and goodwill may be limitless, but time is not. Therefore, a frantically persistent character, a friend, or a person to whom I owe a favor often gets top billing—just as they do with others in public life.

* * *

Spring 1977: Partial Resolution

A crisis treated as a crisis remains a crisis. A crisis treated
as a non-crisis becomes a non-crisis. I'm learning to cool it.
Few mistakes are catastrophic.

* * *

The pieces are all falling together one by one, then faster,
two or three at a time. There is an integration of my selves
that I can't describe. Today at the skating rink the kids'
screams, the erratic music, didn't irritate me as they did six
months ago. My skating feels like dancing. . . .

* * *

Many times I have felt that I—like Alice in
Wonderland—simply "fell" into this position. In my mind I
know this is nonsense; yet I have somehow internalized the
feeling of being incidental and accidental. But my defensiveness is fading; I feel on top of this job, confident and
flowing with its expansive, expanding opportunity, filled
with energy for Colorado and its people.

* * *

Yet, there is no way—no place at all—for me to be totally
separate in perception or impact from my husband, as I was
with a paying job or with a volunteer project of my own. I
can expand, create, produce, learn, and grow. Yet, my true
liberation, my real *growing up*—which was just beginning
when we entered this adventure—has been cut somewhat
short. I can expand until I burst, but I feel little forward
thrust. My steps are purposeful and often successful in the
outer world, but psychologically I continue to march in
place.

* * *

The "stuck" feeling has got to come in part from my
constant and debilitating "checking out" process. All of my
words and actions are weighed for their potential political

effect on the most important person in my life and what he is trying to accomplish. The mental "hoops" I go through create a heavy dependency and restrict a natural spontaneity.

* * *

In life there are cycles of inner growth, expansion, and forward thrust. Perhaps the expanding and learning I am doing now will enable me to move forward faster when my time comes. What keeps me at peace with myself is that my time to move forward on my own will come, and that I will recognize it.

(published in *Colorado Woman Digest*, October/November 1977)

II: Second Banana

For all those spouses married to Top Bananas in politics, art, medicine, business, academia, or life in general—

The attention going to him did not threaten me. What did threaten me was that I was not doing anything. I didn't like being Mrs. Charlton Heston. I was Lydia Clark.

Lydia Clark Heston

Anxiety Lurking in "Second Banana"

By everyone's measure, the weekend was a happy one—packed snow, bright sunny weather, two children who acted as if their parents not only existed, but somehow were salvageable human beings.

V.I.P. day at Beaver Creek, a new Colorado ski area officially opened, featured in "Sports Illustrated," and praised by all. From a former U.S. president to the newest and youngest ski operator, all cogs in the wheel of the area's success congratulated each other with smiles. Smiles. Chatter. More smiles. Jokes. A weekend of public and private acclaim. No booing. No family traumas. Not even a marginal inconvenience.

After each descent from the chair at the top of the mountain, the small groups gathered to exchange stories and vignettes. The snow crackled as the skiers stamped their fiberglass, their wood, and their metal on its polished surface. Poking their poles in the snow for emphasis, they shifted weight from side to side with a kind of stationary swagger. The anticipation of skiing combined with entrepreneurial success created a "macho" aura and demeanor, even in the women.

A good weekend. A great weekend! A weekend I wouldn't have missed. Why, then, the Monday morning blues? Why the exhaustion? The quiet depression? Why the feeling of relief to be home, as if the weekend had been a colossal burden instead of a darned good vacation?

I run to my office as if to embrace its musty clutter. I wrestle, I muse, I reflect, I try to work on an article regarding fashion which somehow feels lifeless, trivial. Good, however, just to be here. Calmer after working, I reflect again on the past 48 hours.

Why was all the smiling, the constant attention so debilitating? Aren't I proud of my husband's success? Yes. Can't I see that I have at least some part of it? Yes. Am I resentful? Sometimes. But isn't he considerate? Usually. Then aren't I just "grousing" unnecessarily? Maybe.

"Second banana." The phrase pops into my consciousness unexpectedly. Second banana. First encountered in a speech by actress Linda Lavin, the term encompasses the stilted passivity syndrome which can suddenly engulf the spouses of notable achievers.

For second bananas, so much time seems to be spent in limbo—waiting, smiling, waiting. A 20-minute wait after the speeches. A 5-minute wait for pictures. At least 10 minutes of socializing after each ride on the lift, foot stamping at the chill when the sun slips behind a cloud.

The governor comes in for lunch. Pictures. Waiting. Lunch. Talk. More waiting. Sunny ski minutes slip away. The family is dancing on a string of the father's position. The children have skied away on their own by mid-morning with my encouragement. But I remain, caught in the middle.

Caught in the middle—sniffing out the social expectations of others as I sniff in the exhilarating air. Would I cause concern or resentment if I skied off alone? Would I even be missed if I skied off a cliff?

Caught in the middle of a three-person chairlift for three long rides between people who talk over my head about issues of only peripheral interest to me. Caught in the middle. I hurry my daughter out of the ladies' room. "The governor is waiting," says the State Patrol driver pointedly, hovering over us as we exit. Big deal, I think, but I say nothing.

In time spent waiting, perhaps only one full ski run was lost. Did it really matter? Not much. The day was pleasant enough to stand and enjoy the view. And a full day of "public relations" on skis can hardly be considered a hardship compared with how most people in the world spend their workdays!

But "second-bananaing" becomes debilitating in any setting when it seems as if it will go on endlessly. By Monday morning, the retreat to the world of words that I alone weave and the attention to letters from readers directed just to me is a welcome respite.

And I wonder about all other spouses married to strong attention-getting others, who not only create their own wavelengths but also find that three-fourths of the world moves with them. How do those spouses survive if they don't have some escape, some activity which is theirs alone?

The weekend. What do I wish could have been different? I smile as I write all of this out of my system. Nothing specific, really. Nothing at all. But a general wish, yes, I do have one.

I wish that someday for some whole 24-hour period, all the "top bananas" of the world would walk in the shoes and feel the psychic vibrations of the "second bananas." Just for a day.

January 12, 1981

"Second Bananas" Reply With Feeling

My column, "Anxiety Lurking in 'Second Banana' " of January 12, 1981, elicited a record-breaking number of letters. Numerous women, and some men, identified with and expanded upon the "in limbo" feeling that can engulf spouses of prominent or dominant personalities. Many empathized with that "caught in the middle" feeling of, on the one hand, enjoying reflected glory, and on the other hand, longing for a more personal identity of one's own.

From a Lakewood writer and mother, formerly married to an opera singer: " 'Second-banana' has it all; all the human elements of dislocation, split-identity, self-pity, fragmentation, awareness that [such a position] isn't enough. My second-banana status hurt like hell sometimes."

From a homemaker and civic leader suffering the "culture shock" of a recent move to a small Arizona town: "Moving from San Francisco has changed my life completely. I live in a goldfish bowl along with being a 'second-banana' which, in itself, is extremely difficult. My husband is president of a local bank, professional banker, educated on the West Coast; we live in Arizona strictly by choice—his."

From a Denver homemaker, educator, and mother of three: "Once again I gave an attentive ear, as he (my husband) told new people the old stories—I know them by heart now. And like you—what do I really wish could have been different? Nothing specific, really. . . . I come home to bed at 1:30 in the morning, cuddle up to my husband of 25 years—and reflect, thankfully, I'd rather be his wife and be second, than be without him and be first."

From an Arvada homemaker, mother of three nearly grown children: "I, too, have had some feelings and thoughts similar to yours. I have struggled with them—thinking they were terribly selfish and ugly. My husband seems to be making great strides in his life and career, but for each notch he gains, it seems that I slip another one back down."

From the wife of a Denver clergyman: "Yes, I bask in my wonderful husband's talent, good looks, and am happy for the adoration he receives. Of course, there are many good times and pleasant moments, but every once in a while, wouldn't it be nice if we could disappear for a day or two? Thanks again for writing about 'me'."

From a Grand Junction homemaker: "Your column on 'Second Banana' hit such a responsive chord I can still hardly believe it. I thought it was all behind me, that I had it all worked out—the depression, the guilt. Oh, the guilt. I guess not."

From a University of Colorado professor: "Some of us work-oriented males need to understand what it feels like to have 'to serve and wait'."

From a Denver entrepreneur and businesswoman: "If that day ever did come when the 'Top Bananas' would trade places with the 'seconds' we'd probably have a revolution before the 24th hour."

Some, however, did not empathize: "If you practiced the creativity and self-esteem you promote in your articles, you wouldn't feel so 'second'." And, from a Colorado voter: "Your husband's job of Governor of Colorado seems to have more than its share of 'bitcher'. Stop feeling sorry for yourself, you could be just a third-rate 'banana' and have something to 'bitch' about."

February 16, 1981

Could You Live This "Perfect" Idyll?

The young woman fell silent and seemed to withdraw. She had been trying to express and explain her restlessness, her vague frustration, as her husband and the other couples at the table looked on with curious amused tolerance.

The woman had just moved with her family to the small resort town in which her husband would become town manager. Her life, to all viewers, especially vacationing city dwellers, seemed perfect. Her two boys could walk to and from school and all their activities. The meadows and streams beckoned them with adventure in the summer, the ski area with new thrills in the winter.

No longer was she burdened with the chauffeuring duties of Denver; her house was small enough to be "done" in two hours (laundry included), after which the day was hers—to hike, to ski, to lunch, to read. Yet, she was bored. She wanted to start her own business, a craft shop or something.

"But the economic situation isn't good enough for that," her husband said quietly, as much to himself as to me, on the walk back to their home. "We don't have the capital to get her started on something like that. Besides her life is—I have to work 12 hours a day—her life's a dream! It seems strange she can't be satisfied."

"Could you?" I thought, but said nothing.

"Could you?" I said again to myself later. Why didn't I ask him. Or better yet, why doesn't she ask him?

Could he be satisfied by that much spare time? Could he be satisfied with no project but a small house to "do" each morning? Would skiing look so good if he could do it daily? Wouldn't he search for something to add more direction to his life—something through which he could make his own contribution?

Despite the fact that more than half of married women now work for pay, the societal expectation that wives will simply fit into a prescribed secondary role still prevails. That they will want nothing more than smoothness to their lives, time away from chores, to play and recreate.

Many women, whose feet hit the floor running at 6 a.m., whose small children, career, and/or housework demands keep them just one step ahead of organizational and emotional collapse till midnight, imagine that nothing could be more of a gift than endless free time. And if by hard work or changing circumstances some women receive that priceless gift of time, they will accept the gift as their due. They will be thankful and they will luxuriate in it. And that's terrific! Yet, many who reach this blessed state may yearn for more. That's okay, too—or is it?

I sit across from another woman friend at lunch. She is starting graduate school, finally. She'll get her Ph.D in psychology and then she'll work for a clinic, and hopefully she will have a private practice someday.

"I finally got through to him," she adds pensively, tenderly, her mood suddenly softening.

"However did you?" I ask knowing of her husband's lack of enthusiasm for her career plans.

"Well, last time he said, 'I can't understand why the money I earn isn't enough—with the house, the pool, the holidays, why you can't be happy with that! After all, you have worked hard to get us here, too, with the kids, etc.; and now they're in school. Why can't. . .?' "

" 'Could you?' I said. 'Could you be satisfied with my life—if you were living it?' "

"What did he say?" I ask her.

"He said nothing," she replies. "He didn't need to—his expression said it all. Suddenly, he understood."

October 5, 1981

Fighter or Not, She Needs Peace

The woman had been a fighter since age 16. "I will go," she said to her father, who was old-fashioned and didn't think college necessary for girls. And she went.

"No," she said to her college counselor when she tried to divert her interest in law to more traditional women's fields. "I will go to law school." And she did.

"No," she said again when law school mentors tried to steer her toward juvenile or domestic courts. "My interest is in corporate planning." And she followed her interest.

"They will," she said to her women's political caucus, when told the "Party Elite" never would accept guidelines mandating 50 percent women at political conventions and child care at all state functions. She, along with others, ramrodded both plans through.

"I will," she said to the senior partners when they did not want her to take time off to attend the National Women's Conference in Houston. She went and they forgave.

"You're wrong," she said to her pediatrician when he suggested putting her baby on a formula because "breast feeding and going back to work in eight weeks doesn't really mix." She made it work.

No question. The woman is a fighter.

Then why, muses a group of her friends in her absence, can't she get her husband to do his share around the house?

"It's the nature of men," says Friend No. 1. "Remember the early feminist leader who said, 'I was married to a capitalist; I was married to a socialist; but neither one took the garbage out.' "

"It's the economic system and financial dependence," says Friend No. 2. "If she made as much as he did, he would do his equal share."

"It's sex," says Friend No. 4. "Remember that the woman's revolution is the only revolution in the history of the world where the oppressed sleep with their oppressors."

"It's the outdated hangover of paternalistic power," says Friend No. 5. "Husbands know they should do more; but it's human nature—not just male nature—to hang on to a good deal until you're pushed."

"Then why doesn't she push?" exclaims Friend No. 2. "For crying out loud, she's moved the whole world outside her home!"

"She doesn't push," says Friend No. 3, with an air of personal knowledge, "because she's too tired. Sure she'd like a bigger hand, but they have only a little time together and he does make her favorite drink. When push comes to shove she won't either push or shove."

"But why?" asks No. 1.

"It's simple," replies No. 3. "When she comes home in the evening from fighting her 10-hour day, she only wants what men for the past century have wanted when they come home."

"What?" asks No. 4.

"Peace," concludes No. 3.

July 21, 1980

Ambitious Women Do Have Happy Relationships, Examples Show

Alicia and I sat down with her friend, Susan, a glowing, intent woman I had wanted to meet. We ordered coffee. Susan smiled brightly, but her eyes were cloudy. As we looked toward her, the tears welled up.

"I think you'll have to excuse me," she said, still trying to smile, the pain in her eyes like that of a hurt animal. She pushed herself from the table, tentatively searching our faces for understanding. "I'm just not doing very well today."

"Can we help?" asked Alicia tenderly.

"No," whispered Susan. She glanced apologetically at me and left.

"She's just ended a seven-year relationship," explained Alicia. "He wants to marry someone else." Somehow I had guessed. An aura of interrupted romance had lingered and mixed with the steam of her coffee, even as Susan had departed.

Alicia took a sip of her own coffee, then sat quietly fingering her cup. "It's hard for women like us," she said thoughtfully. "We're so career-oriented; we're so dedicated, we put men workaholics to shame."

A government relations specialist for a large corporation, Alicia is 38 and divorced. I listened as she began to generalize about her life, Susan's life, and the lives of other women in the super-achiever professional category.

"The only workable kind of relationship for us female over-achievers approaching middle age is the older gentleman with money and position which our hyper-aggressiveness cannot threaten, or. . ."—she stopped for a moment in search of the right phrase—" . . . or a younger man, who bestows many pleasures, but with whom real emotional or intellectual rapport is rare," she continued.

Inwardly, I shuddered. I didn't want to believe such emotional or social limitations exist for women who are cutting new paths for all of us.

"The upward, striving men of our own age with whom we have most in common have chosen or will choose younger women who are more flexible," Alicia added with a sigh as she paused again.

"I do not mean to put these younger women down." She smiled. "Most of them are smart and attractive. Many of them have their own work and do it well, but the work does not dominate their lives. That's what makes them compatible mates. Do you see what I mean?"

I saw. "I'm not so young, but I think I'm one of them," I replied. We both laughed. As old friends we enjoyed discussing our separate and differing priorities and satisfactions. Yet, for Susan we remained sad.

Poet and writer Anais Nin wrote: "There is conflict between my feminine self who wants to live in a man-ruled world, to live in harmony with men, and the creator in me capable of creating a world of my own and a rhythm of my own which I can't find anyone to share." That passage was written more than 30 years ago.

But this is 1979. Is there still really no way two over-achievers can keep a relationship going? Is it competition, lack of energy, or lack of time that interferes? Or is it the age-old sexist assumption that if one person must choose between love and high achievement, it will automatically be the woman?

Alicia and I continued to talk, but by now I was only half listening. Somehow I felt pushed to search for some more optimistic examples than Susan's. Slowly some success stories came into my consciousness:

Marsha is in politics, and her husband, though also in a demanding profession, takes the supportive role. Both have given up peripheral social activities to stay home with their children in the evening.

And then there is Mary, who tells her story in the August issue of *Ms*. Mary and her husband Roger were both professors at the same college. But Mary felt intellectually stifled and accepted a challenge at a college 2,000 miles away. Their one-year-old boy stayed with Roger.

"Our experiment is risky," Mary writes. "We are beginning to stabilize; we can live this way a while longer and still be a family. But we do not do it lightly. We do it only because we need so much to have both halves of the human experience—love and work." (The couple did survive: Roger found a teaching position at a nearby college and the family is together again.)

At one time, feminism may have meant a woman landing a man's job and being super-good at it, while at the same time giving up everything else in life that stood in the way. Now, the liberated woman is more likely to want it all: the success, love, and family life that men, with their wives' help, have been able to combine.

"No one has it all," said a friend when I read him the above paragraph. He's right. And perhaps we have all been brainwashed into thinking that any high goal can be reached without some sacrifice in another area. But which member of a couple sacrifices what and when are now less likely to be dictated strictly by sex roles.

Susan's broken love affair is one of the casualties of change, and there are many casualties like hers. But, at least for some, the stereotypes are breaking down, slowly, painfully, but surely.

One hopes that as more super-achieving couples plan with two career goals in mind, new balances of sustaining love and high-powered work can be attained.

September 10, 1979

Wives and Money: Psychological Aspects

This column is about wives and money. It is not about the dollar amount wives make. It is not about the fact that women still make 59¢ for each dollar men make. Instead it is about how wives' earnings or their lack of earnings affect their sense of self-worth, freedom, and power.

Television personality Joyce Davidson Susskind speaks about the psychological importance of her own earned income in an interview with author Marilyn Funt: "Yes—it feels good. It also has to do with giving it away. You can give your own money away; you hesitate to give away money your husband has earned. Earning your own money is your identity. You are not chattel."

A Colorado woman who has worked outside the home since her youngest child was in the third grade also emphasizes a sense of independence gained from having a career: "Even when the kids were pre-schoolers I did odd jobs for pay, part-time. Some people have a money-working ethic, and I'm just one of them. My income is totally separate from my husband's, and I spend it on whatever I want. Right now I want to help our grown kids launch themselves."

A full-time homemaker and community volunteer, who has quit outside employment, ventures the flip side of the independence dilemma: "I don't feel as comfortable about buying myself clothes or giving to my favorite charities as I did when I had my own paid job, even though my husband's income is now four times what we used to make together. I felt freer when I was working even though we were barely getting it together, and there was hardly any money to spend."

Another homemaker, who has never worked for pay since she married 25 years ago, offers a contrasting perspective: "I never thought of working outside the home, because what I am doing is so valuable. My husband always says he couldn't do what he did if I didn't do what I do. Volunteer work is totally satisfying; my image is not tied up with earning, but with contributing. Neither is my husband's ego tied up with money, though he makes enough."

According to economist John Kenneth Galbraith, the

monetary value of the work done by the average American homemaker is now calculated to be over $25,000 a year. Yet, some women report that their husbands contribute to their feelings of inferiority if they are not earning money, no matter how else they are enhancing home, hearth, and husband's career. Most do not identify with Joyce Susskind's use of the word "chattel," but . . . "My part-time job gives me what I call my 'no more s__t' money," says one wife. "I have some discretionary funds I don't have to answer for."

Although women rail against the value of the dollar as the supreme measure of personal worth, we still seem to become ensnared in the net of using our earned income to measure our value. I fight this mentality, but at the same time, I'm caught. The following is a poem I penned at an Arizona resort a year ago last November:

The buzz interrupts my reading. Damn phone.
Run from the patio; pick it up; it may be Dick.
No, his aide.
The message: "The bellboy may come to move you."
"Why?"

"The room's too expensive;
The hotel is cheating us;
The press is here;
It's state funds—an extra day—"
Troubles to the sky.

I stiffen.
"No," I say. "I won't move. No, I'll pay."
Stiff back relaxed, tension shed like a dream.
My time is valuable—*I'm* valuable—
Artistic, sharp, clean.

"Don't you want to know what it will cost?"
"No, I'll pay. I'll pay."
I'll pay anything not to disturb this day.
One day a year perhaps can thoughts run free.
When the soul can be searched for creativity.

One day a year when the trivial can fade—
Don't bring it all back in some
hand-wringing financial brigade.

Governors are given more room than they need.
We hardly brought luggage—no feasts, or feed.
Yet, we have a kitchen,
two living rooms in orange and red—
When what would suffice is one room and a bed!

So be it. I'll pay—to move, I'd rather die.
Victimized? Yes.
But twice victimized to give in.
To spend the money feels freeing,
liberating, as delicious as sin.
My head is strong—my conscience clear—
My mind is just troubled by one little fear:

If I'd been a wife without my own earnings—
Would I have waffled and swayed:
"Yes, oh, of course.
I'll pack up right away.
What does it matter—
If the move spoils my day?"

May 28, 1983

To Suggest Wives and Politics Don't Mix
Shows Belittling Women Is Still Common

"Wives and Politics Don't Mix," declares the headline of a
column by Jack Germond and Jules Witcover. Naturally, I
continue to read. Which wives? What politics? I'm curious.
The wives turn out to number four; and the "horror stories
about how wife-meddling has hurt campaigns" is verified by
four campaign officials—all male. Hmmm. The examples
are interesting but hardly conclusive enough for such
sweeping generalizations on the negative impact of wives.

I read on. The authors quote Mark Shields, Democratic
campaign consultant: "The ideal candidate is a man whose

wife and family have disappeared on a trip up the Amazon."
Wow! And I thought I was so useful.

The following night I have a dream: I am sunbathing on
that boat on the Amazon. The children are as tan as the
Brazilians on the riverbank. A man on a dock is jumping up
and down waving a yellow telegram; he yells at me in a
Portuguese dialect that somehow I understand. "Your husband's campaign consultant is trying to reach you," he
screams. "You're to come home immediately. The campaign brochure committee needs a family photograph."

"We'll be home after Christmas," I sing sweetly as I blow
him a kiss. As the boat glides on, the telegram fades into a
dancing yellow speck on the shore. Sinking into my deck
recliner, I think of the faceless Washington consultant having a coronary in the phone booth as he dials Western
Union. I laugh and wake up.

Until the dream, I hadn't realized that the article had me
so angry. Why? Perhaps, at the very start, it made me
question how the headline would read if it said: "Husbands
and Politics Don't Mix." Many political spouses—about 10
to 15 percent—now are male. But the whole column, in
addition to implying that wives only could be useless, implied that candidates, somehow, only could be male.

Or possibly the banality of the subject got under my skin.
Naturally there is an inherently competitive relationship
between the professionals who run a campaign and the
candidate's spouse. But is this really news? Fathers and
sons, daughters-in-law and mothers-in-law, sisters and
brothers have inherently competitive relationships. Yet, no
one would suggest that either half of one of these potentially
dueling dyads should be sent down the Amazon to eliminate
the problem. With effort, competitions and rivalries have a
way of working themselves out.

Certainly the condescending tone got on my nerves.
"Undermining" said a friend who also had read the article.
"It undermines not just candidates' wives, but all wives, and
women in general. Racism and religious bigotry have gone

out of style, but it is still fair game to undermine women."

Years ago, before political husbands even approached critical mass, I met the husband of a potential female candidate. "I'm all for my wife winning," he said. He paused. "Although, it is far more important to me that my underwear is still folded neatly in my drawer each day," he continued. Stunned, I mumbled something about his at least being honest. Yet, it would be ludicrous to suggest that this man is representative of all political husbands.

"You'll sound defensive," said an advisor, when I told her I planned to write on this subject. She was right. I do. I don't like sounding defensive. I also don't like giving advice. But I'm going to.

To all campaign consultants: Treat your candidate's spouse—male or female—like a person and not a stereotype. Ask his/her ideas before he/she starts to compete with you.

Possibly you'll become a team.

If not, you'll at least get a family portrait.

April 26, 1982

Some Wifely Thoughts About Politics

"I married my husband in 1963 as a servant," said Ginny Thornburgh, wife of Pennsylvania Governor Dick Thornburgh. " 'Yes, dear—don't get up—I'll do this—I'll take care of it.' Dick did not see me as a servant. I did. But my role has moved from servant to partner. It's been a slow process becoming a partner."

Ginny was speaking to other governors' wives at a seminar on communication and dual career families. "I remember one time when our children were very young. I went to an organizational meeting concerning services to handicapped citizens. Dick took care of the three children in the evening while I was gone. When I came back I fell all over myself thanking him for 'baby-sitting.'

"Then I left the room and thought, 'Why? Why did I thank him for that? He's their father.' So, surprised at my revelation, I turned around and marched back in and said, 'Why did I just thank you for that? You're their father.' His reply: 'Why did you? I didn't ask you to.'

"The real crossroads came at the beginning of my husband's first gubernatorial campaign. I was at a campaign strategy meeting and had about six ideas. My husband jumped on about four of them and told me brusquely why he didn't like them and why they wouldn't work. But the time the meeting was over I was nearly in tears.

"At that point he took me aside and said, 'Ginny, you have to decide. If I treat you like a First Lady with white gloves on, so will everyone else, but you'll have no influence. If you want to be part of the team, you have to be willing to let your ideas be criticized by me or anyone else—and let them rise and fall on their merit.'

"So I decided not to be a pre-packaged symbol, but instead to participate with all of my energy. When he was a lawyer and I was a worker for the handicapped, we moved on two separate tracks, simply comparing notes and catching up in the evening. We have become more of a partnership since politics entered our lives.

"A partnership is not a competition," continued Ginny, who is still an advocate for the handicapped. "I lead from my heart, and he leads from his head. But these are simply lead positions. It doesn't mean that he isn't compassionate, or that I don't have a brain.

"In a real partnership you can choose the area that you want to influence. If you don't choose or if you let others decide for you, you will be phony and you will feel abused. But if you choose, the world is your oyster."

In this strictly private meeting, unencumbered by guests or media, all the governors' spouses spoke freely and from the heart; the lively interchange touched on politics, children, and scheduling, as well as communication and partnership. The following quotes, all of which have been cleared with participants for publication, are further samples of what they had to say:

From Hattie Babbitt of Arizona, a full-time attorney with small children: "I simply don't go out on week nights."

From Sharon Rockefeller, West Virginia: "Your children—they only come around once. Lincoln Day dinners or Jefferson-Jackson Day dinners will come around forever."

From Lynda Johnson Robb, Virginia: "As somebody who has grown up in politics, my mother's advice has served me well: 'Look upon it all as a great adventure!' "

From Honey Alexander, Tennessee: "I was so concerned about the children and how political life might affect them, that I spent all of my time with them. Finally, I realized, 'I have a husband!' I want to be with him, too!"

Again, from Ginny Thornburgh: "Two or three times a year my husband and I go off by ourselves. Not to a fancy place but a comfortable place. Just together without the children. To a cabin with no phone, no TV and no staff."

From Phyllis George Brown, Kentucky: "This woman wrote and criticized me for leaving my baby with a nurse on the weekends I do sportscasting in New York. I wrote back, 'I may change fewer diapers than you do, but I love my baby just as much.' Our keynote speaker spoke of 'fight' and 'flight' as two responses to stress. I'm going to fight. I won't give up my job!"

From Joyce Dreyfus, Wisconsin: "About communication. . . . Find a way to say 'I love you' every day. And sleep in a double bed!"

April 26, 1982

Tribute to Twenty Years of Marriage

Under the category of "profession," my resume lists: homemaker, columnist, television host, psychiatric social worker, politician—in that order.

"Why 'homemaker' first?" asked a constructively critical friend who was urging me to sell my professional qualities more strongly. "How can you say that when you are writing or on TV more than half the time?"

"I don't know," I said, and at that time I didn't.

Homemaker first. I continue to list it first in spite of the fact that I've spent much of my married life proving that I'm not defined by it. I continue to list it first even though I detest some of its more tedious aspects.

I continue to list homemaker, although maybe in my present position I may look phony, pretentious, as if I'm trying to say, "Look, you non-politicized, non-mansion-dwelling, middle-American homemakers of the world, I'm still one of you."

But the real reason I continue to list it grows clearer with time. I think it is because to me it is my primary identity, a grounding. It incorporates parenthood, love and marriage—especially marriage. For in that relationship my spirit is rooted.

I may write about big political issues: ERA, nuclear disarmament, abortion; but it is from my homemaking self, my married self, that the emotional seeds of the articles spring. Maybe "homemaker" suffices because it would be awkward to list "married woman."

My husband and I are very different people. We move at separate paces and we spend energies on divergent things. We work on common goals but are motivated by contrasting objectives. We understand and we misunderstand; we support each other and neglect each other; we love and we argue. Yet, my marriage is where I live first in my womanhood and personhood.

That is why, when his voice cuts through to me in a crowded room, I suddenly wish I were closer and could hear him better, although I've probably heard what he is saying before. That is why I can distinguish the sound, even the vibration, of his footstep as he approaches from afar.

For me, it was not love at first sight, but love at second

sight. On our second date, we watched "Richard the III" on television, talked politics in the park, had a beer on Colfax Avenue, and topped it off with philosophy and cappuccino at the old Green Spider Coffee House.

He was for love, but against the institution of marriage, he said.

I would marry him, I decided.

I did.

And since then, whatever else I've accomplished and whatever sacrifices I've made, that marriage has been my life. As Anne Morrow Lindburgh writes:

"I am married—more than married—dedicated to marriage, and I care about the man I am married to; I care intensely about his life, our life together, his beliefs, our beliefs, his actions, our actions—everything must be worked at without ceasing, all the time. Because he is in it. In the midst of the fire and always will be. And I am so made that I cannot let him 'go his way' and I go mine. No, our marriage is something else."

In this month of our twentieth wedding anniversary, so is ours. And I'm glad.

May 14, 1983

III: I'm Not a Feminist But. . .

For all those women who feel themselves at some stage of liberation—

All that I am, I will not deny.

Joan of Arc

The "I'm Not a Feminist But" Stand Deserves Another Look by Women

I'm beginning to do a slow burn.

I used to be very tolerant of women who said, "I'm not a feminist but—of course, I'm for equal opportunity and equal pay for equal work." After all, it's human nature to want to reap the benefits of progress but at the same time to hold tenaciously to a comfortable self-image which won't be threatened.

I used to empathize when a woman mountain climber reached a new height, reveled in her success, but at the same time dissociated herself from any "women's lib" goals. Why should she associate? Anyone with that kind of ambition, stamina, and courage doesn't need a group of women to get her to the top (unless, of course, she is with a whole team of female climbers!). So why should she parrot feminist ideology if it doesn't mean anything to her?

"I'm not a feminist; I'm just trying to develop my full potential as a woman and a person," I overheard another female super-achiever say last fall somewhere in my travels. With this comment, my acceptance of people's right to claim or disclaim, to associate or dissociate with the woman's

movement slowly began to erode. Although I continued to
smile and nod in empathy, silently and only in my mind, I
started asking questions:

Fine, but what is feminism if it isn't each woman developing her own potential? If that's what you're doing, what is it
about the feminist movement with which you don't identify?

You don't approve of Susan B. Anthony initiating the
drive for women's suffrage? You vote, don't you?

Is it a certain "radical" element that you consider feminist
and with which you don't relate? What "radicals"? The
thousands of women and men who marched peacefully in
Washington for the ERA last summer? The outspoken ones:
Betty Friedan, Gloria Steinem, Bella Abzug? You don't
identify with their style? Their style isn't my style either.
Yet, columnist Ellen Goodman has termed the question of
style a little "tacky" when describing women of such enorm-
ous influence.

And influence they have had. Without those pioneers you
might not have been accepted into law or medical school.
That scholarship you earned just might not have been
available. What? You'll do it all on your own? Of course, you
will get through on your own effort. No political movement
will substitute for your hard work and ability. But your
opportunity to succeed really was paved by others.

Part of my anger may stem from a vague sense of guilt.
Although as affected as anyone else by sex stereotyping and
unequal pay, I wasn't an early leader in feminist issues.
Nine years ago when the NOW chapter started in Denver,
I joined but didn't put myself on the line for anything. I was
having a baby! My priorities were home-centered and
rightly so, but I could have been more active if I'd had the
courage.

Although at the age of 26 I marched in Selma, Alabama,
for the rights of others, it wasn't until 10 years later that I
stood up for my own rights and realized that women, too,
would have to unite to achieve real equality.

I recently read of a 40-year-old mother of four children

who went to work as a flight attendant. "I'm not a woman's libber," she was quoted as saying. For her, a little of my empathy returns. Pursuing a career with such irregular hours, to say nothing of juggling its demands with those of her family, perhaps is enough show of courage for one woman. Her family is supportive of her decision, she claims. Possibly she fears alienating them by coming on too strong.

Yet, I cannot help wondering whether she realizes that 20 years ago she couldn't have begun a stewardess career if she had been over 25; and many airlines would have insisted that she retire once she reached 30. She also would have had to choose between marriage and flying; a choice she wouldn't be prepared to make now.

The simple fact is that many of our opportunities, and those of our daughters (including the daughters of those who have fought so tenaciously against the women's movement) have come about because of a few courageous women with whom we may not feel we have anything in common.

Nine out of ten American women will work at paid employment sometime during their lives. That chance each of us has to become a construction worker, doctor, miner, or factory supervisor may have been won for us by some brash feminist willing to put her job and herself on the line. We don't have to like her, or identify with her, or approve of her style, but let's not put her down.

Most of us owe her a little.

And some of us owe her a lot.

June 26, 1979

Integrity May Be More Important Than Good Manners

Ann, a California woman in her early 40s, is attending a dinner party for 10. During the course of the meal, the guest of honor, a newly published writer in his mid-40s, proceeds to analyze each woman at the table according to his "charm scale." The guests, male and female, hang on the new author's every word.

"Now, Ann," he admonishes, gesturing flippantly in her direction, "is becoming charming, but she's a little too assertive. . . ."

"Too assertive!" I exclaim upon hearing the story. "I hope you got really assertive; I hope you let him have it?"

"I should have," said Ann wistfully, "but I was afraid of ruining my friend's dinner party."

At another party in another state, tall, willowy, brunette, 48-year-old Barbara edges down a hallway toward the buffet line, when suddenly a man she has never met encircles her waist with his hands.

"Honey," he says, "why don't you hustle on in there and bring me a little something to eat?"

"I could have punched him in the stomach!" Barbara fumes later. "But if I'd blown my stack, the scene might have spoiled the party!"

Susan, a Coloradan, age 45, attends an informal social gathering of professional people. Later, she angrily relates an incident: "This woman, the wife of a prominent lawyer, gets on her 'anti-welfare kick.' After she has thoroughly castigated 'welfare cheaters' she launches into how she and her husband, while shopping in a major sporting goods store, turned an ambiguously written price tag upside down and got an $81.00 item for $18.00 Ha-ha-ha-ha."

"Did you call her on it?" I ask.

"No, I felt like the only moralist in the group. There were a few exchanged glances, but most seemed to be enjoying the story and the party. . . ."

In a northeastern state, businesswoman Joan attends her first convention. She enters a packed elevator shocked to hear a group of conventioneers railing about minorities with stereotyped epithets.

"They talked in language I don't think you could have heard in the South in the '40's," she exclaims later, and this is the North in the '80s! "But I didn't say anything," she adds regretfully. "We were going to the same floor and I was afraid we were all attending the same party. . . ."

At around age 40, many of us, women in particular, experience a growing urge to cut through sexism, hypocrisy, and prejudice with a sharp comment. Enough! we think. Yet, because our training, sometimes our whole being, has been programmed for peace-making, bridge-building, and at all costs "saving the party," immediately we are enmeshed in psychic conflict.

In *Passages*, Gail Sheehy refers to the mid-life passage as a stage from which one wants to yell, "No more B.S.!" We don't, of course. At least most of us don't. Our roots are too deep, our social networks too complex and far-reaching to risk sudden rupture by crude profanity. Yet, as we grope desperately through our anger for ways to express ourselves nicely, the moment of truth is lost.

Some women have a knack for easing both personal and group tension with a humorous one-liner which lets everyone off the hook. Others, thinking fast enough and keeping cool, have learned to puncture the inflated balloon of judgmental pomposity with a low-key "I" statement. To say "I am uncomfortable about what you are saying because . . ." is infinitely more polite and at the same time far more effective than to say, "You are a bigoted, insulting, and sexist prig."

Late in the 1960s, I attended a fund-raising party for a candidate for statewide office. A "big spender" attending the party, which was held at the candidate's house, told a loud raucous joke at the expense of a racial minority. The candidate's wife stepped forward calmly. Something in her manner immediately quieted the crowd. "You may have to leave," she said evenly. "We don't allow that kind of talk here."

The "big spender" flushed, apologized, and slid away to the bar. Slowly the party resumed. Later, I heard the "big spender" doubled his contribution to the candidate "in honor of his wife's sensitivity."

Will all such incidents turn out so comfortably for everyone? Probably not. And that's exactly the dilemma which makes "well-brought-up" women squirm. For the worst of our fears can be realized in an instant. Occasionally to save our integrity, we may (shudder) have to abandon the attempt to "save the party."

March 16, 1981

Feminists' Secret Thoughts Embarrass Them

"Well, what can you expect from a bunch of women?" snapped the prominent feminist writer as she looked over the less-than-satisfactory layout of the proposed "Business Women's Handbook," designed by an all-female crew.

There was a shocked silence. "Feminists don't say things like that!" the embarrassed glances of the other members of the group seemed to plead. But the writer remained oblivious to the group's discomfort and to what she had just revealed about herself. The year was 1975.

Feminists *do* sometimes say things like that, I've discovered since. And if they don't say such things, they are at least capable of thinking them.

"I wouldn't say this publicly," confided a close feminist friend more recently, "but I had a twinge of fear when I saw we were flying with a woman pilot. Of course, I reassured myself by thinking surely, as a woman, she must be a *super* pilot," added my friend emphatically, "or they wouldn't have hired her in the first place!"

I'm not as judgmental of such comments as I used to be. It is hard to act "above it all," remembering such parts of my own experience as the time the corporation president with whom I had an appointment turned out to be a woman. "They didn't really give me the president after all," was my initial thought as she entered the room.

"Scratch any traditional woman deep enough, and you'll find a feminist," was one of the rallying cries of the early woman's movement. Often true. Yet, the flip side is also true: Many self-termed feminists find it easy to denounce those who say, "I'm not a feminist but . . ." only to find themselves thinking "I *am* a feminist, but whoops—why did I just think that?" Scratch any feminist deep enough, and you may find a somewhat conventional woman with a stereotyped view of herself and others of her gender.

Regardless of what any American woman labels herself, or the shock with which she may suddenly discover her "opposite side," the duality of certain attitudes she holds simultaneously should not surprise us. Our history is steeped in the conflicting forces of paternalism vs. truly participatory democracy. We all, women and men alike, exhibit our own unique mixtures of both philosophical trends.

Even Thomas Jefferson, regarded by many as our greatest proponent of democracy, exhibited a debilitating blind spot regarding the abilities of females: "Were our state a pure democracy, there would still be excluded from our deliberations women who, to prevent disruption of morals and ambiguity of issues, should not mix promiscuously in the gatherings of men." Abigail Adams, Susan B. Anthony, Eleanor Roosevelt, and Gloria Steinem to the contrary, 200 years later most Americans still embody some of the bleaker side of such Jeffersonian thinking.

"I am a feminist—whoops!" may, in fact, be a sign of progress. If women were to remain oblivious like the feminist writer in 1975, they would continually trip over their own blind spots in their drive for equal rights and responsibilities. "Whoops, why did I say that?" is an honest recognition of the cultural and individual shadow, the internalization of all the images that even today intone that women are somehow less.

Individual and institutional sexism is a part of our heritage. It's too easy always to project its causes onto others. To truly rid society of its debilitating effects, we need first to look to ourselves.

March 24, 1980

Actress Exhorts Women Who Seek Full Equality To "Show Up"

"Show up!"

Linda Lavin, star of the CBS-TV series "Alice," is speaking to a group of about 400 Colorado women. These are the women of the 80 percent—the four-fifths of women in paid employment who work at the low end of the pay scale—in service industries, clerical positions, plants and factories, retail stores and needle trades.

Ms. Lavin is sensitive to the fact that many of her audience might have conflicting feelings about the women's movement. "Maybe you come to this meeting saying, 'I'm not a feminist, but . . . I'm for equal pay for equal work, etc.'" The audience laughs nervously. "Just as I did at one time," says Ms. Lavin. The audience laughs with relief. "But you showed up.

"When you're totally dependent on your job it's hard to rock the boat, to be part of the noisy revolution," Ms. Lavin continues. "But there's a quiet revolution afoot. A revolution which requires that you make one commitment only— the commitment to show up!"

Her message is quietly emphatic:

"Showing up" means going to your union meeting in the evening, even if you are so dead tired you think you can't move.

"Showing up" means taking care of a co-worker's children so that she can attend a workshop that will direct her toward management.

"Showing up" means that you don't laugh at sexist humor or sexual innuendos to show that you are pleasant and easy to get along with.

"Showing up" means attending a discrimination hearing even if the person discriminated against is not yourself.

Ms. Lavin's message is crucial not just for the "80 percent," but for all of us who believe in equal rights and the legal means to attain them. And as we enter a period in which the party platform of the president-elect no longer even pays "lip service" to the passage of the Equal Rights Amendment, Ms. Lavin's gentle command suddenly attains the stature of an imperative.

"Showing up" for a professional woman may mean lending time and practical assistance to a younger woman who hasn't "made it" yet.

"Showing up" for a homemaker could mean going to the neighborhood organization meeting even if she has laryngitis.

Showing up is what the quiet revolution is made of. No noise will have to be made, if only just one half of the 51 percent female population in this country will simply "show up."

On an average, women are paid only 50 percent of what men are paid. "We want what our brothers have, and we have earned it," says Ms. Lavin. How do we get it and other equalities due us? First, we are not intimidated. Second, we make the connection between our personal problems and social issues. Then, simply, we Show Up!

November 10, 1980

Woman in Combat, or Erosion of Equality?

Visual images of women in combat come to me randomly and illogically. A young woman recruit lies injured in a foxhole, her right arm thrown over her head in a futile gesture of self-defense. A fighter plane, with a woman at the controls, lurches sickeningly, spiraling downward to the inevitable fiery crash. The mental scenes resemble World War II movies, starkly drawn in black and white.

Is the vision of a young woman killed or maimed in battle less palpable than the vision of a young man? My rational brain says no. But my heart hesitates. Of course I don't want my daughter in combat; but neither do I want my son in combat. I often feel like the healthy and fit 44-year-old father with four children between the ages of 12 and 20 who recently wrote to a major newspaper, "Don't take any of my beautiful children—take me!"

Admirable women from such differing perspectives as the Mormon Relief Society's president Barbara Smith to seasoned journalist Georgie Ann Geyer make the same argument in different words against female combat duty. If women enter combat, "Who will teach the men, who must be taught to hate, to love again?" asks Smith on the Phil Donahue Show. "Who will relight the candles of civilization?" asks Geyer in her editorial column.

In silence, part of me rejoices when I hear from officials in high places that women never will be allowed on the front lines; that "compelling national interest" will legally supersede any legislation barring discrimination on the basis of sex differences. But the reasons they quote give less cause for rejoicing:

Women have less upper body strength than men.

Women will adversely affect the morale of their own troops.

Women will drive the male enemy "wild" with the need to prove their own "macho."

Separate facilities for bodily functions are difficult to maintain in a combat zone.

Menstrual periods make females weaker.

A sense of forboding intrudes as I realize that these are the same arguments which historically have been used to keep women out of heretofore "men only" spheres:

A woman shouldn't be a heavy equipment operator. Because of her comparatively diminished upper body strength, she should be protected from lifting more than 25 pounds on the job, although children and washtubs remain "acceptable" loads at home.

A woman shouldn't be a police officer; the morale of other officers would be destroyed because their protective instincts toward her will supersede their own survival instincts.

A woman shouldn't be a courtroom lawyer. A male protagonist would be forced to win his case over that of a female opponent to prove himself "a real man."

A woman couldn't be an airline pilot. The cockpit camaraderie of the crew might suffer, and obtaining separate hotel facilities would cost an airline company extra money.

And, of course, a woman couldn't be president! According to Washington, D.C., physician Edgar Berman, the "raging hormonal imbalance" triggered by the onset of menstruation or menopause would render a woman inept compared with the steadfastly rational men who contend for the job.

A persuasive argument against women in combat is that a woman who bears children for future generations should not have to die for her country. The fact remains that hundreds of women in combat-zone support services already have died for their country. In a nuclear war, civilian women would not only die for their country, but *in* their country along with their children and men.

Perhaps it begs the question to say we don't want young women dying in combat. Who really wants any American dying in combat? Still, we should grapple seriously with the fact that the reasons for keeping women off the battlefields could be used subtly and retroactively to erode the agonizingly slow gains women recently have made for equality of opportunity.

Another occasional and irrational vision enters my mental perimeter. One by one, American women remove their surgeons' jackets, their justices' robes, their space suits, their National Guard uniforms, their hard hats. In single file they march slowly into the distant horizon. Where are they going? Home? To lower-paying jobs? The bread line? Oblivion?

This scenario is not in black and white. It is depressingly gray. The landscape is littered not with the bodies of young women, but with their souls.

April 28, 1980

Kramer vs. Kramer: A Learning Experience

Kramer vs. Kramer.

"She left, he did the child-rearing; he should get the kid!" remarks the woman in front of me as we exit (red-eyed) from what is certain to be an Academy Award-winning film.

"The S.O.B.! He did for 18 months no more than what most women do for 18 years, and look at all the credit and sympathy he gets!" explodes a divorced woman friend from Washington, D.C., as we talk on the phone.

"What about the kid?" asks a male lawyer we visit in San Jose, California. "A real court would have taken into consideration the continuity of the child's life."

Kramer vs. Kramer.

The emotional reactions to the movie are as varied as they are intense. *Time* magazine comments, "[The] film offers so valuable a picture of men, women and children of the late '70s exactly because it has avoided polemics." Yet, just because it is so personal, the movie has elicited a veritable landslide of polemic responses from viewers.

Suddenly, I realize that all those who have expounded to me on the subject are over 35. A more important reaction to measure might be that of those in their 20s; the young people described by California sociology instructor Lois McCarty as those "who upon entering marriage, still cling to the traditional values of what marriage and family ought to be, and when reality intrudes, they blame each other."

Young people are seeing this movie in droves. And as they do, I find myself hoping intensely that they will learn certain "lessons" from the "non-polemic" script. Can this movie warn a potential Ted Kramer to resist a tyrannical boss, to not be seduced totally by the shallow victories of the workplace? Can this movie inspire a would-be father to become a real father during the first six years of his child's life? (For, in a psychological sense, Ted Kramer was as absent for his son's first six years as Joanna was to be for his seventh and eighth.)

Can this movie warn a potential Joanna to resist a husband's attempt to outline her life and define her place? Can this movie motivate her to find a second world in which to achieve before a complete break from her marriage is necessary to save her mental health? Let us hope so. Because we "elders" have not spurned "expected" societal norms very easily. And sometimes these norms have paralyzed us.

On a QUBE television show in Columbus, Ohio, 58 percent of professional men questioned said that spending time with their families was more important to them than moving up the career ladder. Yet, the same group of men admitted that they wouldn't make the same statement to their bosses!

Forty-three percent of women with preschool children now work full-time outside the home. Virtually all women want some life, whether paid or volunteer, outside their families, with accompanying recognition. Yet, many women stay in a "holding pattern," denying their own needs, not realizing that personal frustration can be more dangerous to a marriage than individual fulfullment.

"*Kramer vs. Kramer*," says newspaper columnist Joseph Sobran, "shows where love in the real world spends most of its time—not in bed, as Hollywood would lead us to believe—but in the kitchen, the living room, the park— places like that. Love isn't eternal; it's day to day. It brings home the bacon and fries it. It wipes noses. It makes the bed. Sometimes it yells."

Love in the real world is not all in the bedroom; and success in the real world is not all in the board room. Yet, as Betty Friedan states in a *New York Times* article, "The conflicts [between the demands of the work place and the demands of the family] seem insolvable because of the way the family and the work place have been structured in America."

Perhaps *Kramer vs. Kramer* will inspire all of us to take a hard, critical look at this structure and its dehumanizing demands.

January 28, 1980

Why Do We Ignore Half of the World?

One of the housekeepers in the governor's mansion is a short, gray-haired widow in her mid-50s. She is the ideal employee, a quietly competent "angel-in-the-house" with a sunny disposition and a ready sense of humor.

But last week her sense of humor was severely tested by an incident in the State Patrol office of the mansion. There the housekeeper and the patrolman on duty were having coffee with two male electricians who were commissioned for a wiring repair job.

First electrician to patrolman: Can you show us where the upstairs fuse box is located?

Housekeeper: I can. It's on the wall in the laundry room behind the dryer.

Patrolman to the first electrician: I'm not sure. I'll have to locate the mansion's floorplan.

Housekeeper: It's on the wall in the laundry room. . . .

Second electrician to the patrolman: Could you locate the plans soon, or should we just go upstairs and explore?

Housekeeper: IT'S ON THE WALL.

Patrolman, looking at the housekeeper: Looks like maybe she can help you.

First electrician to second electrician: I don't know about the floor plans; maybe we should just go look.

Housekeeper immediately afterwards, still angry: "I told them three times what they needed to know, but only the patrolman began to hear me. This has happened to me before. I know the answer, yet because I'm short, gray haired, or female, I get totally discounted! It's as if I weren't even there!"

The story rings familiar bells. The conscious or unconscious discounting of women occurs in many settings, especially ones which have heretofore been strongholds of men. For example, a woman is appointed to an all-male board. For the first six months she is ignored, her contributions dissipating into the ventilating system with the cigar smoke.

Or, the first female vice-president in a corporation has a new idea for marketing. It is disregarded. Later she finds her idea incorporated into the company master plan. Another vice-president is given credit for it.

It is easy to blame male chauvinism for ignoring and denigrating the ideas of women. And sometimes the blame is justified. Other times, we females need to look closely at ourselves.

Two years ago a group of women lobbied vociferously and successfully to have at least one woman appointed to what had long been an exclusively male state board. "How's she doing?" I asked a member of that board.

"Not too well," he answered. "She hasn't opened her mouth once in 16 months of meetings."

Another female acquaintance complains to me that the men on her committee for soliciting money for a museum do not take her seriously. "I know all about the arts, but nothing about finance," she says. "Money turns me off. So they don't listen." Yet she refuses to learn about fund raising.

In another instance a local manufacturing company sends three representatives from central sales to spend a day at a branch office. One of them, a woman, conducts a meeting for the sales representatives. As she lectures, her two male contemporaries stand in a corner conversing with each other. Toward the end of the meeting the lecturer asks for questions. Each time she begins to respond to a question one of the men steps out of the corner and answers for her. Finally, a saleswoman in the audience becomes annoyed.

"Hey," she says, as she stands up. "Ms. ——— has been dealing with us on these issues all year. We'd like her to answer our questions." Dead silence from the front—but an affirmative nodding of heads in the sales group, most of whom are women.

Does the female lecturer appreciate being praised by an assertive associate and silently validated by her contemporaries?

Not at all. "Oh, that's okay," she demurs, looking coquettishly at the men in the corner. "I really don't mind them taking over."

February 7, 1983

We Like to Bring "Superwoman" Down to Reality Level

When Gone With The Wind was shown on television a few weeks ago, the character of Melanie Wilkes reminded me of a lively dialogue between my high school literature teacher and some female students in 1955. "Melanie," said the teacher, "is a stereotyped picture of goodness—too virtuous to be true; an incredible model of self-sacrifice, untenable as a heroine because her perfection is beyond reach."

Some classmates, the more eloquent of my girlfriends, disagreed. "No," they said, "she is believable. We have to believe her degree of goodness is real—possible if you try hard enough." Although the dialogue itself comes clear and distinct through the years, I'm not certain which side I was on.

The 25-year-old discussion reminds me of the current dialogue over "superwomen." To draw an analogy between Melanie and today's "superwoman" requires a mental leap of some magnitude. Melanie, with her sweet self-sacrifice, could well have served as a "supermom" model for future mothers of the 1950s. But the 1980s "superwoman" model would require the blending of Melanie's selflessness with the goal-oriented, tempestuous, and singleminded character of Scarlett O'Hara.

Superwoman. An attainable ideal? Or just another guilt-inducing "trip" put upon women by society, by men, or (worst of all) by other women?

Columnist Ellen Goodman, who lectured this spring both in Denver and in Colorado Springs, brought howls of laughter from her mostly female audiences when she outlined her version of the 1980 superwoman as we have created her.

Goodman's "superwoman" is a wife-mother-professional who arises each morning at 6 a.m. After a day loaded with mental stimulation, job performance brilliance, "quality" nurturance of her children, and body-shaping exercise, she retires with her husband and sparkles sexually until midnight.

Sure.

We love to bring superwoman down to reality level, and our laughter is therapeutic. But on balance do we gain or lose something when we do so? We want our heroines to be human; but when we find they are, does the revelation let us off the hook and free our competitive energies for our own expansion and development? Or, do we, in fact, accomplish less by not having that ideal embodiment of success to aim for?

A few years ago, I read the book *Working It Out*, a series of essays by women who elaborated on their struggle to achieve professionally and to combine work with other important parts of their lives. One woman's story intrigued me. I liked the way she "worked it out" and rejoiced in the degree in which she had "pulled it together." Although not really expecting to reach her degree of "togetherness," I did, in some ways, make her mental attitude a model for myself.

Later I discovered that an acquaintance of mine had known the essayist in college and had kept up with her over the years. "Things have not worked out so well for her since that essay," my acquaintance said, and proceeded to elaborate.

I wasn't listening. Strange, my quickly successive feelings: first sorrow, then a fleeting, secret, selfish joy at her misfortune, then loss, and then wonder. Do our own capacities to stretch for the stars need our imagined or projected superwoman to stay bigger than life?

I don't know. As in 1955, I'm not certain which side I'm on.

May 25, 1981

A Moral: You Already May Have Raised A "Liberated" Family

"Getting Along in a Non-Sexist Family." I begin the *Ms.* Magazine article by Letty Cottin Pogrebin with considerable trepidation. As with the plunge into any "how-to" article on child rearing, my parental defenses grow up around me as quickly as a magic wall in a Disney cartoon. Depression descends immediately. "Getting Along in a Non-Sexist Family" obviously is a step beyond us. First we must *become* a non-sexist family.

Guilt. I think of all the years when, after each family trip, we yelled to our son, "Scott! Help unpack the car and take the dog for a walk."—never noticing, until Scott recently rebelled, that our daughter, Heather, unquestionably strong enough to help, was consistently traipsing upstairs, toting only her stuffed animal and her small overnight bag.

Guilt. Conversely, when household clutter runs rampant, I, who would engineer a suspension bridge to the third floor before picking up the family junk impeding passage, unthinkingly and repeatedly will delegate to Heather the role of domestic pickup artist.

"Mom," says Heather, interrupting my reading and sitting down on the couch with a determined bounce. "I'm the only *girl* in my fourth-grade class who cares about the Broncos. When can *I* go to a game?"

Guilty again! If she had been a boy, my intuition tells me, we would have had "him" off to a Bronco game well before the age of 9—even if "he" would have preferred to stay home and listen to Beethoven tapes. "Soon, of course," I say as I shrink behind my increasingly intimidating magazine.

"Time for my nap," I say to no one in particular as I yawn and amble, discouraged, toward the bedroom, my parental defenses in a shambles around me.

"Not before you read my fable," says Heather.

"Your fable?"

"Yes, we were studying Aesop's Fables in school, and I had to write my own fable. Here!"

"Once, in Naples, Florida," the fable begins, "there lived a couple of sea lions. The male was picky about his wife. 'Women belong in the kitchen and making clothes for their husbands and families. That's how I expect you to behave,' said he.

Now his wife was beginning to get upset about this. 'Why don't you do the dishes—why not?' his wife said.

'Men aren't supposed to work in the kitchen—you know that,' he answered.

"One day he went out to catch some fish. He saw two married fish arguing and arguing about what men should and what women should do. All of a sudden the couple split up and went in different directions. The sea lion didn't want to split up with his wife, so he went home and told her all about it. He decided women can do anything men can do.

"Moral: Don't be prejudiced against women."

Moral to parents trying to be "liberated": We may be doing better than we think.

October 20, 1980

Will We Ever Be Truly Liberated?

There was a story circulating in the late 1960s that perplexed and puzzled dinner party guests with its implausibility. A father and a son were in a tragic car accident. The father died at the scene and the son was rushed to the nearest hospital for surgery. The surgeon entered the operating room, took one look at the boy and gasped, "My God, I can't operate on this boy—he is my son!"

Who was the doctor? The ghost of the dead father? The boy's step-father? An unrelated doctor who misidentified the patient?

No. The surgeon was the boy's mother. Of course! Not many of us got it in the 1960s. But we'd all get it now, wouldn't we?

I don't know. Sometimes I feel my own liberation will at

best always be unfinished, half-baked, and incomplete. Last summer I seemed to fall into a morass of stereotypical thinking:

I called the emergency room in an out-of-state hospital about my son's painful earache. "Would you have him call me as soon as possible?" I said of the doctor. "Our pediatrician is a woman," replied the brisk receptionist. "*She* will call you as soon as possible." Yes, of course.

Only a week later, back in Denver, I took our new puppy to the vet for a checkup. "Is the veterinarian in?" I asked a white-coated woman at the counter. "Yes, I'm right here," she smiled as she led us to the examining room. Dumb! I thought, so annoyed with myself I tripped over the puppy's leash.

Shortly afterward I was chastised for writing in a column: "Priest, minister, and female counselor." "This way of differentiating assumes that the priest and the minister can only be men," said the female counselor of whom I was writing. Yes.

And I had to laugh when I came to the shocking recognition that a favorite contemporary columnist, C. W. Gusewelle, is a man. Why did I think he was a woman? He writes so sensitively, and in one piece even mentioned something about chauffeuring duties and getting the kids off to school. Wow!

My feminist consciousness is being punished for missing the Colorado-Wyoming E.R.A. march, I moaned. What's the matter with me? Nothing, I guess, except that with all my adult consciousness raising, my formative years were still at a time when doctors and veterinarians were men, priests and ministers were men, and mothers got kids off to school! And maybe, no matter how one grows, it takes time to shake off that conditioning.

As I was returning on a plane from the East Coast recently, my dormant consciousness finally was raised. The senior flight attendant—a dominant, maternal, middle-aged woman—introduced her assistants as the "dear boys who will get you anything you need." Boys! I felt a shock of painful *déjà vu*.

Is there no progress? I mumbled, fastening my seatbelt and remembering my own flight attendant days 20 years ago when dominant, paternal, middle-aged airline pilots would say, "All those cute girls will fill your hearts' desires."

"Doesn't it bug you?" I asked a male flight attendant obviously approaching 30.

"What?" he asked.

"Being called a boy at your age?"

"No," he said. "Why?"

I guess it didn't bother me when it actually happened— only later. No matter the generation, consciousness raising takes time.

November 30, 1981

My "Tortured" Road to Feminism

"Feminists are really tortured people."

The woman quoted, 23-year-old Rachel Flick, stares confidently, hands on hips, from the October 31 issue of the *Denver Post Contemporary* magazine. Ms. Flick is from the new generation of career women; the young women who benefit from equal rights but who hesitate to call themselves feminists. Her negative characterization stereotyping all feminists strikes sharply at my self-image.

I am a feminist. Am I a tortured person? I don't think of myself as one. Often impatient, occasionally irritable, and sometimes decidedly angry. Those definitions fit me. But tortured? No. At least not now. Not anymore. But there was a time when the description fit.

My mind goes back to a Young Democrats meeting in 1963, a meeting at which I had dared leave the designated "wives' post" at the coffee table and join the men and the single women applauding the speaker in the meeting hall. The silent, steely glances of the wives remaining at the table told me they were furious. I had neglected my duty. Yet, where was it written that serving coffee was "wives' work," meeting after meeting after meeting?

Another time in the same prefeminist era my husband and I were planning a potluck supper. "Mike is a bachelor, so he can just bring the wine," ventured my husband.

"No!" I replied, surprised at my vehemence. "We're providing the house and the wine; he can cook something and get it here just like the women will." Doubts nagged at me after my outburst. And fear. Where did that deep exploding anger originate? Was I being petty and unfair? Or, heaven forbid, "bitchy"?

Other disquieting episodes took place at work. As a social worker at the University of Colorado Medical Center, I was assigned a female patient who I determined needed special consideration in scheduling her appointments. She was a foster mother of preschool children and did not own a car. I had a car, so I decided to forego the traditional weekly appointment at the office and visit her at her home.

At the weekly staff meeting I rather proudly reported my home-visit plan to my colleagues. Male eyebrows were raised all around.

"Aren't you being too solicitous of your patient's needs?" asked one male psychiatrist.

"Isn't your patient showing resistance to treatment by not conforming to the traditional hour in the office?" asked another male social worker.

Stunned, angry, and intimidated by the authority in the room, I couldn't find my voice. The strength of my idea was sapped by the subtle vehemence of the male hierarchy. Was my creative scheduling plan for my patient really just letting her off the therapeutic hook as suggested?

Later I lashed out at a male colleague, "Can't you men understand anything what it's like to be a woman? Do you have primary responsibility for your kids? You think all patients are middle-class males with wheels and wives to do the kids' stuff!"

"Hey, take it easy. I'm with you. I agree with your home visit plan," he responded, backing away.

"Yes? Well why didn't you say so at the meeting?"

Why didn't he? Why didn't I? As the only part-time/pregnant/mother/social worker on the staff, I was afraid for my job.

Then one day my eyes were opened clearly, permanently. A favorite male co-worker, passionately involved with the minority community's civil rights drive of the '60s, said to me in a conversation about employment opportunities for women, "I don't see why women need equal pay. Most don't have to work and their husbands support them anyway."

Standing right next to me was another social worker, a widowed mother of two with no income outside of her own wages. Her mouth dropped open. I looked at her. She looked at me. We both looked at him. He didn't seem to see her at all. "You're nuts," I said calmly and turned on my heel.

The next week the organizer for the new Denver chapter of the National Organization for Women called me about becoming involved. "Yes, I'll join!" I said instantly with a sense of exhilaration.

Are feminists really tortured people? Possibly, some are. But for me life was much more tortured back when I saw the burgeoning feminist movement in New York and California as "them" and not "me." There I was, unconsciously a feminist who didn't even recognize I was one. Joining the women's movement validated and provided a vehicle for both my rage and my developing sense of justice.

Since privately and publicly acknowledging myself as a feminist, the rage occasionally still overcomes me.

The torture, however, has faded.

December 6, 1982

Table For One For Lunch

Lunching alone: I have to admit I like it. I've always liked it. It's so simple. Just walk into a restaurant with a book and lose oneself in the meal or the story.

In a life that is often over-peopled, just eating lettuce in silence is a reprieve. See what a pattern the pepper can make on the variegated mixed greens. Slowly munch the celery and mushrooms, and savor the spicy dressing. Eavesdrop on conversations that have no relationship to your life. Make up your own story about that intriguing-looking couple at the table in the corner.

This habit of lunching alone started back when I was a flight attendant. Eager to try any highly rated but low-priced restaurant, particularly in New York, I soon learned that if I waited for the right escort to show up, or the right flying partner to get through with her long-distance phone call to her boyfriend back home, I could starve. So I went alone—always armed with a book or a magazine to put off unwelcome glances. And I've never been hassled in a res-taurant. My desire to be alone must shine like a warning beacon.

During my husband's first campaign for the governorship, I would treat myself to a lunch out as a time to get my thoughts together for a speech. Through the slow ingestion of a good meal, I felt I was equipping myself for the "battle."

Last winter while in Washington, D.C., I took a long leisurely meal at the restaurant in the National Gallery of Art. The pasta salad was average, but I luxuriated in each noodle. I studied the pamphlets on the Rodin exhibit, and literally entered 19th-century France. I tried to imagine the life of the sculptor Rodin who was not even accepted by the Parisian artistic academies until he was 37 years old.

A few months ago *Ms.* magazine ran an article on lunching alone and how to handle it, pointers on getting up the nerve to enter a restaurant alone and techniques for diffusing any potential problems. I couldn't believe it! There was a part of women's liberation I had learned on my own, hoofing ahead of the herd rather than stumbling to catch up.

So much else was a struggle. I had to be liberated from "when are you going to quit work and be a *real* mother?" I had to be liberated from "ring around the collar" and "get your diapers whiter than white." I had to be liberated from "a good woman keeps her own counsel; don't trouble his mind with your concerns."

But lunching alone came naturally by the age of 22. I'm at lunch now, pencil in one hand, fork in another. If you're watching me, I'm ignoring you. If you feel like socializing, I'm sorry—not now. Maybe we can have lunch together . . . tomorrow, or the next day, but not today.

April 12, 1982

IV: The Emerging Woman

For all those women who are growing and changing and have found friends to grow and change with—

I live at a turning point. There are more books now than before in which women tell the truth.

Louise Bernikow

The "Emerging Woman" Symbolized Process, Not Goal

The Emerging Woman. It's a phrase that has reached its zenith. In contrast to the phrase "liberated woman," it suggests neither political activity nor abruptness of movement; it says similar things but in a softer way.

The Emerging Woman. The three groups that have asked me to speak about her in the past year have included that exact phrase in the wording of their invitations.

To Emerge. Webster's dictionary defines it as: "To rise from or as from an enveloping fluid," or: "To come out into view; as the sun emerges from eclipse."

Emerging is a process, not a goal. It reflects evaluation rather than sudden change, a slow series of steps as opposed to a drastic denial of one set of values for blind adherence to another. Perhaps it is liberation in its truest form.

A friend of mine emerges from her home every day at 9 a.m. She needs to finish her doctoral dissertation; just being in her own home has become an onerous distraction. The creaking floorboards intrude on her thought process, reminding her of necessary repairs. The phone rings incessantly; the plants droop and seem to cry out with thirst. So, she rents herself a small office. As the children depart each day, she determinedly pedals off to her quiet space.

Another friend emerges from the nursery as the last child turns six and enters the first grade. She goes to school, too—as a teacher. She does not do this suddenly or with abandon. She has been preparing for it for 10 years by grading papers in her field and by keeping up with educational literature.

A third friend, at age 30, emerges from what she now calls the "scheduled frenzy of professional life" and immerses herself totally in motherhood. "I've had all that! I've proven myself in the big world," she says with a relaxed sigh as she settles back in a large beanbag chair with a cup of tea. "These babies, which I had never expected to have, are now my life."

A fourth emerges personally, though physically she stays in the same place. She is a homemaker who remains at home, but she has changed her attitude. "A year ago I was drowning in my home," she says in disbelief. "But my depression was really from self-imposed expectation. You know that 'get your shirts whiter than white' TV ad mentality. I actually bought it! Then I thought I could pay someone to do that stuff if I went back to work. That made me think of what-the-heck I was doing at home anyway. When I realized it was not to maintain a perfect house, but to nurture my kids and to provide a warm home for my family, I began to change."

For this friend, the emergence has been shakier. To change oneself without changing one's actual physical environment takes a special kind of courage. Each expectation of family, friends, and self has had to be scrutinized. Sometimes the process has been painful.

Emerging is an intransitive verb. Liberated is something that can happen to you. But you can't be "emerged" by anyone else. You can only emerge yourself.

The late '70s woman doesn't let household clutter or office chatter keep her in her "place." There are no excuses, and no places in which to be kept. Her territory can include home, office, factory, school, or all of the above.

When she comes up against a brick wall, she neither cowers in fear nor is impelled to break it down. Instead, she analyzes its obstructive quality like a technically trained mountain climber. It may take minutes or it may take months; yet eventually, she will emerge over the top of the bricks, the rising sun at her back.

October 8, 1979

Success Is a Conflict for Some Women

I sit on the wooden porch of a mountain cabin, pen and paper in hand. The ideas are slow in coming. Perhaps the view of the Gore Pass Wilderness Area distracts me, or maybe it's the distant muted hammering which indicates even more condominiums will dot the green, rolling hills. I shudder. More houses everywhere, I think. I also think it would be nice to be able to buy one.

Yet, the visual and auditory disturbances don't quite deceive me into thinking that they are the cause of my distraction. Instead they seem more like a convenient something upon which I hang my avoidance of work. My father's voice comes out of the past. He catches me daydreaming and grins, "What have you done constructive today?"

I have been eagerly anticipating this time alone to work uninterruptedly. As spring slowly unfolded, I could almost sniff the mountain air from Denver. I recall Virginia Woolf's essay, "A Room of One's Own," and I marvel at the importance of such a simple thing as physical space in helping one develop one's thought. Today I have that space.

Yet, much more seems to be needed to get the mind cranking. The old-fashioned word would be commitment. But somehow it doesn't quite fit. As women, most of us are committed, but to whom or what? We are so well trained to orient ourselves toward others, we have a way of distracting ourselves even when "they" are not around. We wonder: did the shirts get to the laundry? The movie money to the kids? The dog to the vet's?

In their book, *Working It Out*, Sarah Ruddick and Pamela Daniels phrase with clarity a female pattern of avoidance. "Many of us have become preoccupied with finding space and time to work only to discover that, once alone, we turn anxiously away from the empty canvas, the blank page, or the un-photographed scene."

Are we afraid of failing? Or succeeding? Possibly, we fear both. If we are propelled into the work force for financial reasons or some other factor beyond our control, we sometimes are frightened that we won't make it. Yet, if we choose to work independently because we want to, are we frightened that we will be so successful that we will have new responsibilities, new expectations, and a new self-image to maintain?

Or is it possible that we simply fear our individual work itself? Succeeding, failing, or the more likely probability of landing somewhere in between may not be so frightening as the fact that we do concentrated work at all. To work hard with a specific goal says to others, "I am."

Possibly I make too much of all this. Being distracted in the mountains can't be exclusively a female trait. To concentrate on another dilemma of women in our society is perhaps the biggest avoidance of all. If I blame, and/or succumb to, the unique mental barriers of women, I have a great excuse to do nothing forever!

Yet, the psychological-societal issues are real. They are historic in a country that until the present day has emphasized the nurturing skills of women almost to the exclusion of other potential skills.

In an essay called "The Sacred Fire," poet Celia Gilbert reveals her personal fear of work most succinctly: "To give myself to my work—to admit that I loved it as much as husband and children, needed it as much . . . was the most terrifying admission I could make."

Again, I hear my father, and the fathers of others of us who were preadolescent girls immediately following World War II. "Women should be highly educated in order to be the best wives and mothers possible." To attain this education for their daughters, many of our fathers made large sacrifices. They were proud of their progressivism; and they were progressive for their time!

Yet, our ambivalence may stem from those often unintended double messages in our upbringing which said to us: "The values of hard work and enlightenment are important for you girls; but they are important only to the point that your work and enlightenment serve your families."

So we do come with conflicts. "I have an inner need to produce" is a scary thing for a woman, especially a married woman, to say. We forget that ours has always been a work ethic, product-oriented society. For a man to make a plain statement about his psychological need to work would sound ridiculous, not because it isn't true, but because it is so true that to state it is unnecessary.

July 16, 1979

Job Title No Longer Frightening

"What do you do?"

It's the inevitable cocktail party question. It's smashing when you can shoot 'em dead with "I'm an animal trainer for Barnum and Bailey!" or "I'm a foreign language interpreter for NBC news." But 99.9 percent of us aren't either, nor do we have the chutzpah to look the friendly interrogator straight in the eye and tell an outrageous lie.

"What do you do?"

If one is primarily a homemaker, to answer honestly can be agonizing. "To describe myself as a homemaker is a put-off," says one friend, "though I don't mean it to be. People move away in a hurry as if afraid I'm going to launch into a discussion on diaper rash. I'd rather tell 'em I'd just

finished Barbara Tuchman's *A Distant Mirror*, but that
sounds showoffy."

A homemaker may "do" more than anyone else at the
party, but capturing the essence of what she does in one
definite phrase is the challenge. Fifteen years ago at such a
party, before our children were born, I asked a homemaker
with children what she did in her extra time. "Oh, nothing
that anyone else would be interested in," she said with full
confidence and went on to something else. "She didn't even
try to justify herself!" I said judgmentally to my husband
later.

Seven years and two children later, I was asked the same
question; and with a pure, conscious wave of pleasure and
relief I gave the same answer. How wonderful finally to be
comfortable with my choices and not have to defend them.

But it was a long and torturous trail to that degree of
comfort. Right after my first child had been born, I went to
work part-time as a social worker. The multiplicity of my
new roles provided a plethora of pleasing answers to all
cocktail party questions:

"Are you breast feeding?"

"Yes."

"Are you still working at your profession?"

"Oh, yes!"

"But, you're home most of the time?"

"Yes."

"Even giving dinner parties?"

"Yes."

It was the answer to every woman's dream. I could say yes
to everything and please everyone without lying. Terrific!
Except for the fact that, still in a post-partum daze, I secretly
was terrified and felt inadequate both at work and at home.

"What do you do?"

It's a superficial question reflective of our society's way of
measuring a person by title or performance. People don't
ask me much anymore. They know what I do or they think
they know, so we leave it at that.

Yet, the problem remains for many, and homemakers are coming up with some creative answers. Lynda Bird Johnson Robb's answer to the doctor's question, "What do you do when you're not being a momma?" was, "What do you do when you're not being a doctor?"

"What do you do?"

"I am a domestic engineer," quipped a personal friend.

"I'm a family life planner," replied another.

"I'm a teacher in a special school for two children," said a third.

"Not one bit more than I have to," retorted another with a big smile.

"I'm a full-time wife and lover," said a homemaker with no children.

Okay, so creative ways to answer the question are possible when one is nondefensive. "What do you do?" is a limited conversation opener with most of its askers bearing no malice. And far worse openers exist. For example: "What does your husband do?"

October 22, 1979

"Here I Stand": A Key Phrase For Real Living

She might stand at the kitchen sink waiting for deliverance from household chores. Or she might sit in her office waiting for promotions. Like a pilot in a holding pattern, she appears to be circling her life, looking at it through the fog, but unsure of which way to direct it. Hesitant to land on any one spot, she is reluctant to say, "Here I stand."

Not limited to one occupation or station in life, the woman in the holding pattern can be encountered at political picnics, volunteer clubs, homemaker groups, professional networks, union shops and various charity luncheons. She is neither feminist nor antifeminist, nor does she attempt to define herself as "somewhere in between." In short, she does not define herself. She usually is married; she might work inside the home, outside the home, or both. She often is described by others as successful, cheerful, cooperative, and patient. She does not rock the boat. Usually she is popular. Often she is unhappy.

Who is this vaguely dissatisfied woman, and what keeps her in her holding pattern?

Marabel Morgan, author of *The Total Woman*, might say she is not "total woman" enough. If she will teach herself to love and obey her husband more, she will find her contentment through total submission to her man.

Jungian analyst Irene Claremont de Castillejo might propose that she is discontented because her "suppressed masculine archetype" is turning its force inward and has no purposeful or creative outlet in her life the way she is living it.

Betty Friedan, in her early writings, might have said if she happens to be a housewife, of course she's unhappy; homemaking by definition is stultifying. She needs to get out and get a job.

But that stultification does not have to exist, Arlene Rossen Cardoza would say. Cardoza, who published *Women at Home* in 1976, promotes the home as the ideal workplace. It contains all the elements of being one's own boss, flexible hours, and a plethora of opportunities for creativity. The only problem with being a homemaker, suggests Cardoza, is when a woman has no peers nearby, or when she feels that homemaking is not her own choice.

And perhaps it's the degree of choice a woman perceives and asserts that makes the difference. The woman in the holding pattern is passive rather than active. Often a dependable employee, she is capable in terms of follow-through but is devoid of a central purpose, a frame of reference, or a central goal from which related and even nonrelated activities can flow.

"I find I take hold of life differently if I treat every alternative as a choice, even if it isn't one," a woman in my support group recently said. "Right now I'm thinking consciously about how I spend my time and making a mental note of whether I really want to do something. I can't always do what I want, but I can at least know what I want."

A subtle shift of perspective distinguishes self-actualizing people from their more passive counterparts. The self-actualizers are known not so much by the choices they make, but by the fervor with which they pursue their choices and by the fact that they become active participants in their own behalf.

Some people appear born with this assertiveness. For others it takes an event or a set of circumstances, an inspiring teacher, a death, a birth, one's own birthday, marriage, divorce, a dramatic shift either way in one's financial situation, or even the passing comment of a friend.

Self-actualization has its liabilities. Once one says, "I am," or "I choose," one opens the door to possible failure and disappointment. Visualized choices might not be real choices after all. And historically, choices for women have not been as broad as choices for men. Because society has not only accepted but encouraged passivity in women, a woman might feel more comfortable in viewing herself as having no free will.

Yet few people in totally passive mental states are content even when they appear successful and cheerful to others. The American idea of free choice is historic. Despite its illusory quality for certain groups at certain times, it has waxed and waned its way from the 1770s to the 1980s, and its continual presence has made permanent inroads on the consciousness of all of us.

The woman in a holding pattern might be terrified to land on any one spot, but if she keeps circling she doesn't really live at all. If she views all reality as choice, she might be brought up short; but if she views herself as having no choice, that can become her reality.

June 30, 1980

With Everything, There Are No Guarantees

Run-away wife: there she was, in full color on the cover of a national magazine. Suitcase in hand, the young woman was firmly shutting the gate of the white picket fence. It was obvious she was leaving home for good. Her smile, even in the still photo, seemed to be ignited by the click of the gate.

I read the accompanying article. More women, it said, were running away from their suburban homes, the onorous household chores, and the husbands on whom they had become depressingly dependent. Instead, they would "do their own thing" and make their own money in the big city.

The year was 1969. I mused about the woman on the cover. Her life would surely be different, but was it somehow bound to be better? I doubted it. Yet, there was a Norman Rockwell romantic feeling to the picture. The woman's smile carried the radiance of a promise, a dream to come true.

Her departure would bring complete happiness in independence, the photo seemed to say. Hmmm. Yet, hadn't it been just a decade before that the magazine cover photos, with the woman ensconced securely behind the fence in housedress and high heels, had promised complete happiness in domesticity?

Two different dreams, a new "package" and an old "package," yet the same magical expectations. It is now 1979, but many of us still seem to be lured by the idea that if we just find the ideal situation, life will be perfect. Women once thought marriage was the be-all and end-all of their lives' goals; that the ideal husband would bring automatic lifelong happiness.

The feminist movement brought us alternatives, yet some of us embraced the new choices in the same unquestioning way we had previously clung to the old ones. All we needed to do, we thought, was to buy the new package and follow the tenets of liberation. We would secure equal or superior paying jobs in a man's world and zap! fulfillment would be instant.

In the September 25th *Rocky Mountain News*, Linda Bart from Sterling, Colorado, wrote of the fallacy of the feminist dream. As a convert to the new package, she wrote: "Today I am all those things that seemed so right in the early 70s. I am a professional woman. I live alone and know how to change the oil in my car and fix my plumbing. . . . I am also reaching a point in life where my career isn't as fulfilling as I thought it would be. I no longer sneer at housewives; I look longer at children in the supermarket.

"I am not questioning the equality of women and never will. I am only questioning the changes in so many lives the [feminist] movement has brought. I also have to question the loneliness."

I, too find myself questioning her loneliness; yet, for Ms. Bart and many others, a more painful and incisive question may be this: Why is it we can be so easily seduced by a promise? Instant happiness won't come from a feminist idealogue riding a white horse anymore than it will come from a knight in shining armor. But we dream on.

The surest thing to come from the choices offered by the women's movement isn't instant happiness, but more choices. And our happiness won't be instant. Whatever paths we choose, happiness more likely will come slowly, as a byproduct of hard work and a certain amount of luck.

There are no guarantees.

Poet Celia Gilbert bought the first "package." She was the woman behind the white picket fence. In her early marriage she gave up her poetic dreams; they took her mind off homemaking and thus evoked feelings of guilt. In her essay, "The Sacred Fire," she writes of her adherence to the package of perfect wifehood and motherhood; and how her faith was shattered by the loss of one of her three children:

"Death had broken the old covenant by which I had lived, practicing the magic of my mother and generations of women before her; the belief that a single-minded preoccupation (with homemaking and nurturing) would be recompensed by the survival of my children, the barter of a life for a life, renouncing mine for theirs."

Boston Globe columnist Ellen Goodman urges us to beware of the latest "package": "The ad people, having used up the sales possibilities of the feminine mystique, are now selling a feminist mystique." The ad people are implying, of course, that feminism means having it all, doing it all and controlling it all. The feminist mystique is "superwoman" in triplicate!

Goodman cites a cogent example of the latest "package," a *Psychology Today* advertisement for the memory phone by Code-a-Phone: "While Virginia Clark prepared a gourmet meal, she called her office, her husband, the pharmicist, the pre-school, the hairdresser, the babysitter and all the members of the bridge club, with the touch of a button." Virginia Clark, of course, is a slim, gorgeous, professional-appearing young matron with every hair in place.

Will we buy this superwoman package, just as many of our men are entering the kitchen and the nursery for a share in both the domestic joys and burdens? Will we prefer pushing all the shiny new buttons ourselves to asking our husbands to dial a babysitter on a plain, old-fashioned phone?

And if we buy this latest package and manage everything ourselves, will we wonder why, though we now "have it all," we are lonelier than ever? We have come of age and should know better. Run-away, stay-at-home, or superwoman: there are no guarantees.

October 29, 1979

Support Group Members Are More "Comfortable"

Comfortable. It's the only word that comes to me as I survey the varied faces of my woman's support group which has been meeting for 10 years. As I look around the casually

pillowed living room floor of our monthly meeting, I try to
remember the first time we met.

Self-consciously "into" consciousness-raising, we were
then not so comfortable. Small scenes of the first meeting's
drama persevere over the years. The players, whose real
names don't appear, included Gina, who was "into" advice-
giving: "If you'll just do this and this and this, everything will
turn out OK. . . ."

Barbara was "into" hysterics. Although no "crazier" than
the rest of us, she had a predictable floor-prone semicon-
scious fit each session.

Jean was "into" equality. If a woman reported doing
something supportive for her husband, Jean would query,
"But would he do that exact same thing for you?"

Marty was "into" crying "on cue." As a social worker, she
knew that "feelings" would get the group moving.

Ada was "into" sexuality.

Greta couldn't stand unhappiness.

Billie was so angry, she couldn't stand joy.

Earnest, serious, and groping, we pursued our own iden-
tities as relentlessly as the men we often criticized pursued
the "God of Success." Twenty of us then. Ten dropped out
over the years, and a few more dropped in. Now, a dependable, comfortable group of eight to twelve.

From self-conscious to comfortable in 10 short years.
Does our increasing age account for the evolving comfort?
Or has our increased ease evolved from the fact that the least
comfortable have left the group? Was it perhaps the very
struggle of self-conscious search which eventually allowed us
to mellow and blossom? Or was it the continual strengthen-
ing of our feminist beliefs, running concurrent with the
steady softening of our tone, which now renders us more
secure?

Actually, it is all these, but there is something more,
something in the times. Not in our age, but in *the* age: 1980s
women simply are more comfortable with themselves.
Other sources confirm this sense of ease.

"We couldn't have done this 10 years ago and been happy, satisfied, and reluctant to leave a group that consisted solely of women," wrote Ann Schmidt in her *Denver Post Contemporary* column about her recent 34th college reunion. "We were raising no consciousness there. Some of us had careers, some had spent their lives being housewives and mothers in the best McCall's tradition. But, there was no envy or regret, no display of upmanship. We were for the most part comfortable with who we were and what we had become."

Comfortable.

Another *Contemporary* article from the *Los Angeles Times* examines the agility with which women now unite the feminist with the feminine. "Ten years ago we might have been a consciousness-raising group, but now there is nobody in that group who needs it," says Bobbie Greene Kilberg of the Aspen Institute about her women's group in Washington, D.C. What do they talk about? "Whose kid knocked a baseball through the neighbor's window, or who has been to Disneyland lately," says Kilberg.

Shopping for clothes, talking recipes, or joining a Neighborhood Hospitality Club are activities which no longer seem unfitting for the image of a business or professional woman making her mark in her field. And why should they? To be truly liberated is to not need to conform to anyone's mode—old or new.

On the weekend of June 20th, I will give a speech at the American Home Sewing Guild and lead a march for the Equal Rights Amendment within the same 24-hour period. Ten years ago I would have been uncomfortable—possibly in conflict, mentally searching for which activity reflected the "real me." Today it's simple. Both of them do.

June 15, 1981

The Social Penalty of Adulation

A well-known psychoanalyst remarked to the woman with whom he was lunching, "I answered your letter because I knew if I had a meal with you it wouldn't be just another 'open-mouthed lunch.'"

An "open-mouthed lunch," the woman explained to me later, was the analyst's definition of lunching with someone who was so in awe of him she just sat there with her mouth open during the whole meal.

The mental picture made me laugh, albeit nervously. Immediately I was wondering how I acted when around someone I admired. When in a state of adulation there is a tendency to go to extremes: to talk too much, over-praise, and gush; or conversely to be so careful, measured, and intimidated that one is downright dull.

The episode started me thinking about the times that I'm in awe: seldom with political people, nor great scholars, nor artists, partly because I do not aspire to become them, nor could I. "Position" as such does not impress me, maybe because I've met enough average people in elevated positions to be skeptical.

But, give me a chance to meet a writer, a journalist, especially a woman—a Tillie Olsen, an Anne Morrow Lindburgh, a Madeleine d'Engle—whom I may admire and whose skills I would emulate; lead me to someone with whose activity I am "ego involved," and I can become immobilized. I wouldn't be competitive with a tennis player or a figure skater, because that's not where my ambition lies. *Where my ambition lies.* That phrase perhaps is the key to the deformity of a potential relationship. A particular episode comes to mind.

Suddenly, I was sitting beside a woman whose likeness I craved to be. Yes, I know that Ralph Waldo Emerson said that "Envy is ignorance . . . imitation is suicide." And that the Bible says, "Thou shalt not covet," and Leo Buscaglia says, "You are the best you. You always will be the second best anyone else." I know all that, and I believe. And, yet, for a while I forgot.

Although too sophisticated for the "open mouth," too many times annoyed, myself, by the super-charger or over-praiser, not wanting to eulogize, or antagonize—"You are so great! How do you get your ideas?"—and not honest enough to simply say, "I'd like to write like you do," I felt stiff, unnatural, and stuck to my chair.

I even forgot all the amenities of conversation that can open doors to relationships—children, geography, food, recreation, and politics in a nonpartisan sense. Instead, I became a frozen replica of the person I always twitch to get away from: careful, measured, dull.

Agh! The fog of ambition-intimidation that can veil potential human connections—as the smog obscures the sun!

November 16, 1981

Casual Housekeeping Attitude Proves Inspiring

She was about 45, warm and pleasant, pretty with an inner radiance not related to striking features or artful makeup. I liked the informal way she served supper (unselfconsciously asking her husband to help) and whisked the remaining food away on a portable table when the meal was over.

She didn't fuss about my inability to eat much. She was secure enough in her hospitality to believe me when I explained that it wasn't the food but my travel exhaustion that caused my loss of appetite. Neither did she fuss at her 5-year-old boy who played quietly with the cat and a stack of cards under the large round living room coffee table on which we ate.

While our husbands tackled the latest crises in the Middle East, we talked quietly of child-rearing and family therapy. She is a psychologist and recently has published two books. I could tell she was talented in her profession, not by her publishing record, but by the warmth and acceptance with which she addressed her own four children.

Although this home was in a foreign country, we had common interests and a common language. It wasn't surprising that we related easily to one another. Yet, there was something more. Trying to analyze why I felt so superbly comfortable, I let my eyes wander over my surroundings. Teenagers' coats were dropped on chairs. The 5-year-old's trucks and stuffed animals peeked out from under bookcases. But it was when all the family games crashed out of the coat closet that I knew my hostess and I could be real soulmates. As we all laughed, I silently vowed to be more like her; upon returning home I, too, would adopt a more comfortable attitude toward casual housekeeping.

Because as often as I have tried to kill it, there resides in the back of my brain an immaculate, superwoman ideal, a self-contained, computer-like woman with no loose pieces, the epitome of perfection and efficiency. This resident ideal is a super-woman who pursues her own career, spends quality time with each child, and in her spare moments keeps a shiny, spotless household that is at all times ready for guests. She, of course, has no help and is so organized she never needs to set priorities.

Since my level of organization falls far short of that of my resident ideal, I do have to set priorities. When the housekeeping goal is the one to go, my resident ideal becomes a larger-than-life, polished, soap-crazed, guilt-producing TV ad lady. Holding her latest detergent in her perfectly manicured hands, she scowls at me with a look that clearly says, "You'll never make it!"

Not surprisingly, my latest political position has thwarted my determination to kill this ideal and free my spirit. Since the first floor of "my" house is kept impeccably clean (by others!) as a historical tribute to Colorado, I often am seen by the public as Mrs. Superclean. Because visiting friends do have the habit of journeying up to the private quarters, I constantly am tempted to at least try to live up to this super standard on the upstairs level of the house as well. Is this really necessary? I'm beginning to doubt it. And my foreign friend is helping me.

Here, miles from home, was an obviously accomplished woman who with no apologies whatsoever could allow new guests to observe a comfortable amount of clutter. As we had been invited (by her husband) at the very last minute, her casualness made me feel more welcome as she had sacrificed none of her day on a rushed attempt to impress us with a house-beautiful portrait.

She obviously was more interested in us as people than in what we would think of them or their surroundings. That attitude is a rare compliment from a stranger! And partly through her willingness to reveal herself through her environment, she becomes an inspiration as well as a friend.

May 7, 1979

V: Parenthood

For all those people who are "blessed by the tie that binds": children—

God, give me the strength to endure my blessings.

source unknown

The Elation of Being Alone (at Last!)
Is Overshadowed by a Lonely Feeling

Well, it's finally here. That long-awaited, much-anticipated, and over-planned five days. The week in which the columns will be written, books will be read, the body will be tuned and tanned, and any interruptions, will be purely self-imposed.

Husband and son are rafting on the Green and Yampa rivers with like-minded fathers and sons. Daughter is visiting friends "with a pool of their very own!" in Arizona. Even the weather cooperates. Warm enough for early-morning jogging in shorts, but cool enough for sunbathing at noon without frying. With a slight breeze and no smog, each day dawns clear, and stretches ahead in a straight, uncluttered line.

The silence in the big house is deafening. Somehow, it is different from the winter silence after they have all slammed out the door to office or school. The jogging is spiritless in spite of clean air and the chirping birds. It's as if sneaking in those short runs before the kids wake up is what makes them fun. Sunbathing brings forth irritability and red blotches, not relaxation and smooth bronzeness. Who wants the sun when the whole day is available in which to take it? The pungent taste of breakfast sausage has lost its edge. The books to be studied for a Great Books course seem less than great. Reader's block and writer's cramp set in.

A "blue funk" my husband would call it. More like a mild state of mourning, it seems. But what is being missed or "mourned over"? The answer is obvious.

Much has been written about how young children can sap the energy and creativity of their mother, leaving her as drained and useless as a dried sponge. More has been written about how husbands, even helpful ones, make incessant inroads on a wife's time and consciousness. Men simply like things to move on their "own wavelengths." And it's true. All true.

But other writers, and even the same writers, have begun to show the opposite side of the familial coin. Husbands and children can be a positive force for creative work. What they bring in human experience is immeasurable. And the fact of their mere existence causes one to focus.

Singer Melba Moore elaborates on the fact that marriage and motherhood provide the emotions that she brings to her work: "If you only live showbiz, what do you have to bring to showbiz?" she comments in a *Denver Post* feature article.

Author Barbara Grizzuti Harrison follows a similar track when she writes in *Ms.* magazine about the year her children went to live with their father. "The 'aren't you lucky they're gone' people say, 'now you can work undisturbed.' What I'm not sure they understand, what I'm not sure I've always understood, is that I might not ever have done any good work at all if it had not been for the fact of their existence."

And columnist Ellen Goodman writes of her own revelation upon returning to work after her infant daughter was born. "Suddenly I was no longer, in some recess of my mind, working 'until' I had a child. Whatever had been tentative about my commitment became solid. If I wasn't doing this 'until' it was time to do it better."

Three years ago when my family left briefly, I penned a short verse. Again, the words fill my mind:

Away from that family
My thoughts flow unhindered
My rhythm is strictly my own
Yet, the presence of that family
Renders solitude creative
Without them, I just feel alone.

July 14, 1980

It's Sheer Truth: A Mom Hears Better

The mother was slowly awakened by a clip, clip, clip sound. At first, as it penetrated her sleepy unconscious, the noise wasn't disturbing. But gradually the sound evoked a vague sense of urgency, then a mild prick of alarm.

Half resentful in her stupor, the mother roused herself and peeked over the railing of the balcony guest room to the living room below. There, wielding 12-inch shears, was her 3-year-old son methodically clipping off the leaves of her hostess's favorite plant. Fifteen feet away sat the child's oblivious father, mentally devouring the Sunday paper, cup of steaming coffee in hand. She should do something, she knew, as she gripped the railing of the balcony. Yet, she was struck dumb.

"You sleep in; I'll watch him," her husband had said the night before. The reassuring words pounded mockingly in her ears. She *should* do something. Her son could hurt himself. Yet, he didn't seem about to. And the plant already was pruned beyond repair.

"It's all in the uterus," this mother had been told when her first child was born. "You will hear his every sigh and gurgle in the nursery 20 feet away because you carried him in the womb so long. The mother-infant bond remains distinctly physical even after delivery. Your biological instinct guarantees the survival of the race." The theory had fit her freshly awakened maternalism and she had believed it.

"No, it's all in the society," the mother was later told by feminists in the early '70s, right after her second child was born. "Women and men are not that different. Mothers are trained to be in tune with their kids. They are the ones at home, so they learn through the experience. Fathers would be as adept if they had the same degree of practice." She had believed that, too. Yet looking at the living-room scene below, she wondered why. Two children and years of experience later, and he still is untrainable, she thought of her husband.

"It's really because you're superior," was the latest message she had heard on maternal instinct. "You can be everything a man is, but the richness of your motherhood experience will make you 'more' in everything you do. Your children distract you not because your concentration powers are inferior, but because your humanness abounds. You may not produce as much in your work life as a man of equal training, but what you do produce will be of higher quality, womanly quality, motherly quality."

Now "into" post-equality feminism, the mother believed that, too. Why not? The theory was by far the most ego-gratifying. Yet, right now she wished, fervently, that some men (one especially) would become equal in that much-touted maternalism.

The mother stood still. All the reasons she had been given for her maternal sensitivity had passed through her mind in less than a minute. By now her son had shorn the plant of all foliage, adeptly relieving himself of the scissors without injury. He climbed onto his father's lap.

"Hi," said the boy.

"Hmmm," said his father as he hugged him and kept on reading.

The young mother then remembered a passage she recently had read when browsing through Richard Restak's book, *The Brain: The Last Frontier*: "Female infants are more sensitive to sounds—female babies are also more easily startled by loud noises. In fact, females' enhanced hearing performance persists all through life."

So, it is biological after all! But motherhood isn't "all in the uterus"; instead it centers itself in the Eustachian tube. A child's sound that eludes the consciousness of a father awake will penetrate the brain of a mother asleep, simply because her gender has been endowed with enhanced hearing ability.

The mother believed that, too, now. How simple, she thought, as she climbed back into bed and pulled the pillow over her ears.

March 3, 1980

Tread With a Lighter Step and Your Child Will Answer

Sometime between Mother's Day and Father's Day, my children always ask, as I asked my parents, "When is Children's Day?"

"Every day is Children's Day," I answer them, as my father answered me. "The world is made for children."

Yet, I think of our son's furrowed brow (he does not share his thoughts) or our daughter's tears (she shares them easily). For each of them, a day is a milestone accomplished, but for us the days can slip by unnoticed into years. We adults sentimentalize childhood, forgetting that each minute is lived intensely.

Children cannot put themselves in our place, I think; yet, can we really put ourselves in theirs? The uniqueness of each child's experience is precious and fragile, easily threatened by parental criticism, over-investment, or even praise.

Our daughter plays her latest piano assignment with skill and aplomb. I am struck dumb. We are a nonmusical family; I can hardly pick out "chopsticks" myself. *You will be famous one day*, says my voice of parental aspiration. *See how good you can be when you practice?* says my voice of perseverance and morality. But, *wait*, says my voice of discretion.

I remember the words of the late psychologist Mark Rudnick, who trained me to work with children at the University of Colorado Medical Center: "Praise is better than criticism; but don't overkill; don't co-opt a child's experience and immediately make it yours. Don't talk too much when a smile, a wink, or a hug will suffice." I kiss the top of my daughter's head as she plays on.

Our son thinks of nothing but scuba diving; at the dinner table he rattles off the exact percentages of oxygen, nitrogen, and carbon dioxide that are inhaled and exhaled at a variety of given depths under water. *See how well you learn when you apply yourself; now, if you would only do that with your school work. . . . If you study hard you will be a marine biologist; Stanford, of course, has the best program. . . .* Again, I stop myself. Leave the experience intact; he'll come to those conclusions himself; and if he doesn't, he just may come to better ideas of his own. Across the table, he sees his father's proud grin—reward enough for now.

So often we think of child rearing as providing feedback, setting limits, pointing direction, giving advice, chauffeuring to and from, and teaching from our own experience—all of which it is.

But it is more than that, or, perhaps, less than that, if "less" means listening more carefully and treading with a lighter step. To paraphrase Kahlil Gibran in *The Prophet:*
"Our children are not our children . . .
We may give them our love but not our thoughts.
We may house their bodies but not their souls,
for their souls dwell in the house of tomorrow."
If every day is Children's Day, it is because children live each day with more creativity than we do. May parenting be not so much the passing of our own torch of wisdom, but the kindling of each child's unique flame.

May 26, 1980

Mother's Day Is When Your Family Shows Love
Mother's Day just barely will be over by the time this

appears. My breakfast will have been cooked, perhaps brought on a tray to the bed. And maybe—just maybe—the remainder of the day will involve nothing more complicated than soaking up some sun.

A proud day, a special day. A day which would hurt if I were forgotten. But in some ways, a superficial day. For my "real" mother's days come at other times—unannounced, spontaneous as a breeze.

In thinking of "Mother's Day" and the rewards of motherhood, I reread my journal from last August on Cape Cod:

It's cold; I am dozing and reading in front of the fire. Suddenly the screen door slams. My 9-year-old daughter Heather stands before me, hurt and enraged.

"I didn't get *my* horse! I have to ride in the carriage. Scott just got *my* horse! It's not fair!" she cries.

"But, Heather, he isn't your horse; you rode him this morning; it's Scott's turn this afternoon; that does seem fair."

"But I want him!" Tears.

"Things can be sad without being unfair," I murmur as I stroke her head. She wrinkles her nose. "Let's read *Little Women*. I don't want to go if I just ride in the carriage."

"Okay."

She snuggles in on the musty couch by the fire and hands me the book. "You read." I begin where Jo gives her account of reading to demanding Aunt Josephine. Jo, bored to distraction with the stories, says:

"I gave such a yawn that she asked me what I meant by opening my mouth wide enough to take the whole book in at once."

"How could Jo swallow a book with a yawn?" asks Heather.

"I don't know, should we try it?" I hold the paperback to her mouth.

"Mom, how stupid!" she says disdainfully, then giggles. We both envision Jo swallowing the book as she yawns.

"Oh, her poor stomach!" Heather rubs her own stomach, dramatizing sympathy.

We read about Beth and her dolls. "Beth cherished them (even the old and the ugly) all the more tenderly for that very reason and set up a hospital for infirm dolls. No pins were ever stuck into their cotton vitals; no harsh words or blows were ever given them; no neglect ever saddened the heart of even the most repulsive; but all were fed and clothed, nursed and caressed with an affection which never failed."

Heather feigns tears. "Are you crying about the poor dolls?" I ask.

""No, I'm crying because I broke my favorite fingernail."

"Why was it your favorite?"

"It was so pretty, and it's the only one I don't bite."

"A girl old enough to care about a pretty nail should be old enough not to bite them," I lecture.

"Let's read," says Heather, her eye still on her finger.

I continue. "If anybody had asked Amy what the greatest trial of her life was, she would have answered at once, 'My nose.' "

Heather sits up straight. "I know; it's like mine; too small; I hate my nose! Mom, if I had a twin would she look just like me?"

"She might."

"Nose and all?"

I try to explain the difference between identical and fraternal twins.

"So, she could be very different from me?"

"Yes, in fact, she could be a he."

"You mean my twin could be a boy?" I nod.

"Forget it!"

I continue to read. "When Amy was a baby, Jo had accidentally dropped her into the co-hod. Amy insisted that the fall had ruined her nose forever. . . ."

"Mom, would twins get sick at exactly the same time?'

"Hmmm. I don't know. Maybe they'd have to be invaded by twin germs."

Dottie Vennard with Grandmother Mabel Walton in her garden. Portsmouth, N.H., 1940.

Dottie Vennard with younger sister Jane and their dog Waggo in front of home in Palo Alto, California. 1948.

Dottie on her new bike. Palo Alto, 195

Dottie (right) with freshman year roommate Kay Brown (left) and friend Allana Crothers (center). Occidental College, Los Angeles, 1955.

Dottie's father, the late John K. Venna 1956.

Dottie Vennard (top right) with members of United Airlines stewardess class at Brown Palace Graduation Ceremony in Denver. August 20, 1959. *Ralph Morgan.*

Wedding photograph after the marriage of Dick Lamm and Dottie Vennard (center). Tom and Lynette Richardson (left) and Paul and Judy Striker (right) attend. First Unitarian Church, Denver, May 11, 1963.

Dottie accompanies husband and candidate for governor, Dick Lamm, on the Boulder to Louisville segment of his 888 mile campaign walk. October 1973. *Denver Post*.

Heather Lamm, 3, collects balloons the night of the primary election, September 10, 1974. "My daddy winned!" she told reporters. *Rocky Mountain News*.

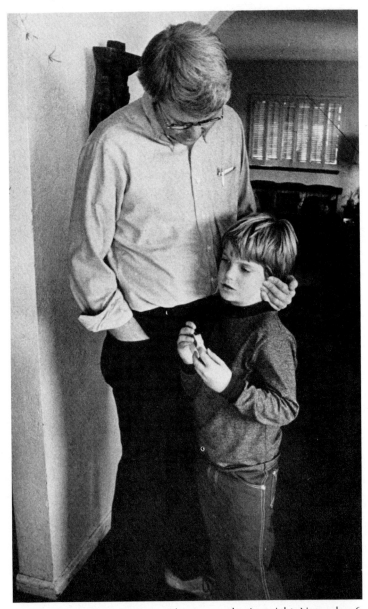

Dick Lamm comforts Scott, 6, at home, on election night, November 6, 1974. *Denver Post*.

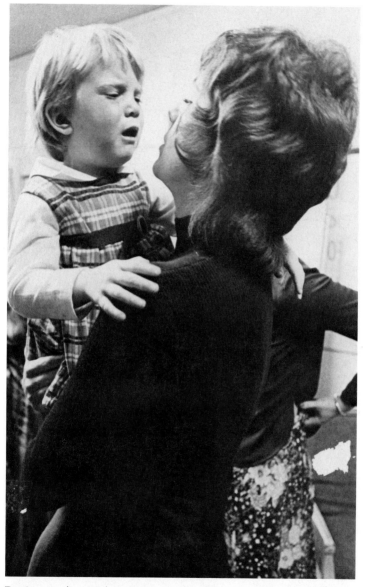

Dottie consoles Heather, 3, at Lamm headquarters as the vote count goes on. November 6, 1974. *Denver Post*.

The Lamm's first house at 531 Emerson in Denver just before they bought it in January 1964.

The Lamm's second house at 2500 South Logan, Denver. It was purchased in the fall of 1967, just before the birth of their son Scott.

View of the solarium of the Governor's Mansion. The house was built by Walter Scott Cheesman in 1908. It became the Governor's Mansion when it was given to the state by the estate of the late Claude Boettcher and received by Governor Stephen McNichols in 1960. *Russell Ohlson.*

Dottie approaches the family's move to the governor's mansion with apprehension. Former first ladies' pictures adorn wall in vestibule. January 28, 1975. *Denver Post.*

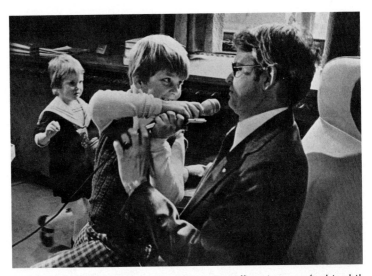

Newly elected Governor Lamm takes some office time out for his children, Heather, 4, and Scott, 7. Inaugural Day, January 14, 1975. *Denver Post.*

Dottie Lamm visits the Urban League Child Care Center in Colorado Springs, spring of 1976. *Linda Eichengreen Sutton.*

Scott and Heather Lamm open a Kool-Aid stand by the governor's mansion. Their faces reflect the slowness of the first day of business. July 1975. *Rocky Mountain News*.

Dottie cools off as she judges entries in the "Anything That Floats" contest on the South Platte River. September 1975. *Denver Post*.

Judy Henning, Dottie Lamm, and Bonnie Andrikopoulos smile from the top of Pike's Peak after leading 63 members and guests of the Colorado Commission on Women up the mountain for a centennial/bicentennial celebration of Katherine Lee Bates' trip up the Peak in 1893. It was from Pike's Peak that Bates was inspired to write "America the Beautiful." July 1976. *Marilyn Holmes.*

Dottie gets Scott, 8, and Heather, 5, ready for the Centennial Climb of Mt. Evans, August 1, 1976.

Dottie and Dick take a short sprint after the Governor's Cup race benefitting Governor's Council on Physical Fitness. October 1978. *Rocky Mountain News.*

Dottie does a little pre-election campaigning after Governor's Cup race, October 1978. *Rocky Mountain News.*

Dick and Dottie arrive at Lamm campaign headquarters on election night to thank workers for the governor's victory in his campaign for a second term. Dorothy Vennard (Dottie's mother) is at left. November 7, 1978. *Denver Post.*

Lieutenant Governor-elect Nancy Dick, Governor Dick Lamm, and Dottie Lamm celebrate the governor's election to his second term and the Lieutenant Governor's election to her first term at the victory party at Democratic headquarters, November 7, 1978. *Denver Post.*

Dick, Heather (8), and Dottie Lamm celebrate inaugural events with Mary and Arnold Lamm, the governor's parents. (Scott, 11, is home with the chicken pox.) January 1979. *Rocky Mountain News.*

Former First Lady Betty Ford and Dottie converse at the 1979 Carousel Ball to benefit juvenile diabetes. June 9, 1979.

Dottie, on weekend leave from the hospitalization during which she found she had breast cancer, consoles Heather on a family outing.

Scott, 13, and Heather, 10, visit Dottie in her Rose Hospital room where she is recovering from breast cancer surgery. September 1981.

Students from Westview Elementary School in Northglenn deliver a get-well banner to the governor's mansion prior to Dottie Lamm's return from the hospital following surgery. Holding the banner are: (left to right) Bobby Barros, 11, Kelli Bruning, 11, Mrs. Parr, Mark Sherman, 11, and Lori Ann Siminas, 11. September 1981. *Denver Post.*

Dick and Dottie Lamm attend annual Carousel Ball. October 1981.
Denver Post.

Jane Wells-Schooley, 1981 National Vice-President for Action, N.O.W.; Mary Estill Buchanan, Secretary of State; Doris Durdy, Chairwoman of Colorado Women's Political Caucus; former First Lady Betty Ford; Polly Baca Barragan, State Senator from Colorado, and Dottie Lamm pose for photo after E.R.A. Countdown Rally in Denver, Colorado, June 1981.

Members of the woman's support group to which Dottie has belonged since 1971. Top row, left to right: Lissa De Andrea, Jan Temple, Dottie Lamm, Ann Ewing, Stuart Cornwall. Bottom row, left to right: Connie Platt, Kathy Bond, Carolyn Medrick, Judy Goldberg. January 1982. *Denver Post.*

Lieutenant Governor Nancy Dick, Dottie Lamm, and Dick Lamm celebrate the governor's election to his third term and Nancy Dick's election
to her second term. Behind the governor is Nancy's husband Dr. Stephen
Barnett. To right are Security Agent Ray Elder and Campaign Manager Jim
Monaghan. November 1982. *Denver Post.*

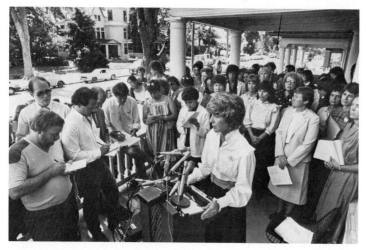

Dottie Lamm speaks at a rally staged in front of the National Organization
of Women's Race Street headquarters in Denver. 150 men and women
protested the light sentence issued by Denver District Court Judge Alvin
Lichtenstein to convicted wife-killer Clarence Burns. June 1983. *Denver
Post.*

Heather, 12, Dick, Dottie, and Scott, 15, pose with family dogs, Carmel and Travis. July 1983. *W. Russell Ohlson*.

"Twin germs! What would they look like? I know, like little black bugs wearing twin hats." Heather dissolves in uncontrollable giggles. "Twin germs! Gotta go—the riders are back."

The door bangs. The room is suddenly empty and silent. No human sound. Just the crackling of wood in the fireplace. I doze and read intermittently. Suddenly, I feel a quiet presence beside me. "I know you are sleeping," Heather whispers. "I just played tennis and I was awful. But I picked you some flowers on the way back."

Flowers on my pillow. A light kiss, and she is gone.

Mother's Day—last August.

May 11, 1981

Like Father, Like Son—Unless He Belongs to You

"But you only said they had to be *clean!*" exploded the boy in mock indignation as he looked at the gaping holes in the knees of his dark blue corduroys. His father clenched his fist, gritted his teeth, and let out a long sigh ending with a loud "ach!"

"We'll talk to him later," said the boy's mother.

"You bet," groused his father, who moved to the party's bar.

A twinkle in the boy's eyes said, "Gotcha!" The boy knew his father wouldn't drive him home from the elegant party to change his pants. He knew, since it was dark and far, his father wouldn't make him walk. And since he was only 12, of course, he knew he couldn't drive himself.

The boy also knew his father far better than his father understood. The boy had just come back from his grandmother's house where he had heard "the old plaid jacket" story.

The old plaid jacket had been a favorite of his father's at age 14. The family was on a two-day trip to a cousin's wedding when his mother had discovered the jacket in her son's duffle bag. Fearful her son would disgrace the family, the youth's mother had stuffed the jacket in a garbage can behind the motel in which they were staying.

But the 14-year-old was an early riser. While exploring the vicinity of the motel that morning, he had discovered the jacket. After smuggling it to the wedding, he had donned it secretly in a dark alcove of the church. Triumphantly, he escorted guests down the aisle, wearing the wrinkled, garbage-stained jacket and a defiant grin.

Remembering the old plaid jacket story, the 12-year-old boy reminded his father of it as they returned home from the elegant party. "That story has nothing to do with you," said his father, still mildly irritated but mellowing.

The next night the father was dressing in his tuxedo for the "All Charities Ball." "Are you really going to wear your cowboy boots with your tuxedo?" asked the boy's mother.

"You bet," said the father. "The invitation only says 'black tie.' It doesn't say I have to wear dress shoes."

At the dance, the boy's parents met an impeccably dressed 18-year-old son of some friends. He appeared impeccable—that is, until his ascent up the stairs revealed bright red tennis shoes under the perfectly creased formal dinner pants. "What class," exclaimed the boy's father as he laughed and slapped his knee. "I admire a young man who can pull that off."

"If he were *your* son, you'd kill him," remarked the boy's mother.

"You bet," said the father.

                                      February 12, 1980

Book Evokes Apprehensions of "The Empty Nest"

The living room stereo blares "Girls, Girls, Girls" from "The Merry Widow" and the record winds down to its end. The morning cartoons chatter and scream from the TV room. But, aside from the electronic noise, it's quiet for a Saturday.

Our son lies on the couch with a blanket. He has a touch of

the flu and, uncharacteristically, doesn't feel like teasing his sister. She in turn has empathy for his illness and leaves him alone. She sits quietly in a rocking chair, stroking the guinea pig we are boarding for the summer.

I'm catching up on the Friday newspapers. In the *Denver Post*'s *Living '79* section I read an excerpt from Terry Hekker's new book, *Ever Since Adam and Eve*. The piece is titled, "Mother's Regret: Time With Children Flew Too Fast." Ms. Hekker speaks of the empty-nest syndrome and the joys of having raised four children. It's an old subject, but somehow she covers it in a fresh, appealing way.

Suddenly, I'm weeping uncontrollably. I stop, just as suddenly, more surprised than sad. Me? Crying? About this? I'm many years away from the empty nest, and just yesterday I was counting the days and hours until school would start in the fall. But Ms. Hekker is reaching me. Why?

Older women have preached to me about the empty nest before. When our second child had a 104-degree fever at the age of 10 days, and our first one was fulfilling his role of the jealous 3-year-old by spreading fireplace ashes on the living room carpet, these women would smile indulgently. "It all goes too fast," they would say.

Huh! I would think, as the advice-givers marched off to their jobs, yoga lessons, or bridge parties. But it does go fast. And perhaps that's why I now hear Ms. Hekker loud and clear.

In another chapter, she writes eloquently and tenderly about babies. Again I'm touched, although I'm years away from that stage, too. Her passage, ". . . babies have no proper necks, but there is a place right behind the ears and down an inch where head meets torso that is heaven to nuzzle," brought tears to my eyes and warm memories to my mind which even old photographs of myself in such nuzzling scenes fail to evoke.

Ms. Hekker stayed home full time as she raised her four children, a choice she admits isn't open to all. But her

chapters must appeal to all mothers because they come from
her own experience and don't preach. She doesn't say, "you
should" but simply, "I did." And she humorously admits to
the hardships of homemaking as well as its joys. "In rearing
young children there are times when going to work as a
piano mover or a steel furnace stroker does appear to be the
easy way out."

Sometimes Ms. Hekker and I disagree. For dramatic
effect, she occasionally pits feminism against traditional
homemaking. I find this polarization a dated interpretation
of philosophies and roles which are by no means mutually
exclusive.

Yet, she defends the choice of full-time homemaking in a
way that it needs to be defended, not as a burden to be
endured, but an exciting, rewarding option which deserves
higher status than our society gives it.

She has touched me at a pivotal time. I'm right in the
middle of child rearing (11 years from the first birth and 10
years from the second high school graduation). As our two
children march into school this fall, the part of me that wants
to hurry the clock recedes, and the part of me that wants to
slow it suddenly grows larger than life. Although, at least on
that first day, they will each look fine and will have forgotten
nothing, I already want to yell, "Hey, wait a minute!"

August 27, 1979

Even Mothers Can't Fight Mother Nature

"Two, Four, Pinch, Pinch, Pinch."

"It's really very easy," said my self-confident 10-year-old
as she instructed me on the care of her menagerie. Two
mealworms for the turtle in the tub; four mealworms for the
turtle in the dishpan; three pinches of fish food for the
guppies in the tank; one pinch for the goldfish in the salad
bowl.

Easy? I look apprehensive. She reassures me; it's only
two weeks. "Mother, you'll do OK!" she says as she snuggles

under the sheets for her last night at home before summer camp. "And besides, you know all about the guinea pig and the hamster!"

"Two, Four, Pinch, Pinch, Pinch," I mutter as I leave the room. Oh, Lord, I pray, please don't let any of the animals die before she returns.

With a sinking feeling, I recall the guinea pig we kept for the school last summer. My daughter had just returned home alone from a plane trip to her grandmother's. I was at a conference in Aspen. The desk clerk interrupted me with a small piece of paper which read:

To: Mrs. Lamm
Caller: Heather
Time: 1:05 p.m.
Message: "Her guinea pig died."

Full of anger and sadness, I raced to return her call.

My feelings tumbled in turmoil as the staccato ring went on interminably. It must be the housekeeper's fault! No, it's my fault! I accepted the "summer boarder"! Ornery animal, how dare she expire; she was so shy, so cuddly, so apparently healthy. How could any such trauma occur when I'm not there. Damn it anyway!

Heather answers the phone: "Mom, my guinea pig died."

"I know."

"Mom, I don't know what happened. She was sick when I got home, and I called the vet to see what to do; but when I returned she was dead."

"Oh, honey, that's awful."

"I know, but we did all we could. And the teacher says she was old when we got her."

"Oh."

"Mom, we're coming up to the mountains to see you and we'll be there in about four hours! I love you. See you soon. Bye."

As I hang up the phone, a whole new set of reactions beset me. There is pride, she handled it so well. And worry, but is her reaction appropriate? Don't kids even grieve over animal deaths anymore? Is she hard-hearted, or, heaven forbid, "repressed"? And fear, she's only 9 years old and she doesn't even seem to need me. Damn it, anyway—calm down!

A week later I phoned the teacher who owned the guinea pig. "Of course, I understand," she said. "Our children need to understand, too. That's why we keep animals in the classroom. The children need to learn that death is a part of life."

The children? How about adults? Was she speaking straight to me? I felt awash with relief. Presently the same sense of relief soothes me again. I'll do my motherly best for my daughter's animals but will stop assuming that I, even as "Mother," can control everything. Whether I'm home or away, nature occasionally just may have to take its own course.

Remember now—Two, Four, Pinch, Pinch, Pinch. Yes, and a few prayers, too.

July 6, 1981

The Grudging Giver

My daughter's feet are growing. Not unusual for an 11-year-old child in the middle of a growth spurt. Not unusual but maddening. Her feet are growing not only out of her shoes, but out of her rental ice skates. One can't rent skates past size six, and this means money. Money for skates which she will outgrow in six months. Money for a second pair if she takes freestyle as well as figure skating. Money—right after we bought her a ski outfit, the price of which made my head spin in spite of the 30 percent spring discount.

Maddening, those feet. I'm taking it personally. As I start breakfast, I stomp around mumbling to myself, mentally flipping through the checkbook. My mood is sour and my love less than motherly.

"Heather," I catch myself saying as her one eye opens to the clock radio. "Heather, get up and clean your room. You've got to do your share after all we do for you. Look at that new ski parka on the floor. Now we've had to spend a lot of money on you and your interests. . . ." As her one eye quickly shuts and she pulls the blanket over her ears, I find myself transformed to another bedroom 30 years or so ago: I'm spending the night with my best friend Jan; in fact, I spent many nights with my best friend Jan. And each morning, her mother, divorced, harried, and needing to be off for work before we arose, would stand at the foot of Jan's bed and lecture.

The words varied with the day, but the message was always the same: how hard she worked, how lazy Jan was, how much money they didn't have, followed by a long list of chores that Jan would grunt and groan her agreement to as she pulled the blanket over her ears just like Heather. Guilt with a capital G. Jan's mother even made me feel guilty for existing. Imagine what she did to Jan. I had vowed I would never be that type of mother.

Yet here I am, spouting the same poison! I look at myself with a critical perspective, and the shock of recognition mellows the venom. "Wake up, honey," I say gently, "we'll talk later."

"Grudging giver," I brand myself and immediately dislike the label. Begrudging one's giving—that's what parents need to avoid. But shouldn't a child learn to clean her room? Of course she should. And to take care of her things, especially high-priced items? Of course. And shouldn't a child be taught the value of money, taught to understand that a whole family is supporting her skating, skiing, or soccer talents with more than love? Of course. And occasionally she should be asked to help pay for her own clothes or activities.

But she should learn those monetary values as values in themselves—tools to prepare her for life—not as a result of "Look at all we do for you, you ungrateful wretch."

A child should never be given everything he or she wants. If financial sacrifice is impossible, then we ought not to make it. If a time sacrifice is too difficult, then we should deny it. But when we make the decision to support a child's activity, let us enjoy our investment and encourage the pursuit of high goals. Begrudging one's giving is worse than denying the gift. "Look at all I do for you," is a negative bond that teaches a child little but resentment. So what's the matter with me anyway?

As my daughter trudges off to school in her soon-to-be-replaced "tennies," the growing of her feet doesn't seem so irksome anymore. At least I'm not taking it personally.

March 27, 1982

Self-Flagellation Can Hurt Your Kids

Our 5-year-old did not seem sad when he left on the bus for day camp in 1972. Rather, he appeared in a daze. He hoisted his little pack and joined the rest of the kids without looking back. He hadn't even started kindergarten, but for eight weeks of the summer he would be gone from his home six to eight hours a day.

Around the middle of the camp term I received a call from the counselor. "Scott doesn't seem to be involved in what we are doing; he goes on his own track and seems to be waiting to come home each day, even though we have arranged many fun activities."

As she spoke, my repressed guilt at sending him away resurfaced. I was no longer working outside the home, yet our daughter was a year and a half old and I had hardly spent a moment with her alone. Heather needed time to blossom without a dominant older brother. Certainly, I thought, a good day camp was better than sending Scott to a daily sitter in town. I had wanted it to work out for everybody. But it didn't. Now, when our son shows the normal insecurities of adolescence, I sometimes reach back to that summer and blame myself.

Heather was ready to go to nursery school by age 2½. But the bus ride was a problem. We had two cars, but the gubernatorial campaign staff in 1973 needed one of them and my husband needed the other. Every Tuesday and Thursday I would wait for Heather on the corner to make sure the bus driver let her off safely. Each time she would fall into my arms exhausted. An hour's bus ride each way was simply too much for a 2½-year-old. But we didn't have the means to change the system.

Between the ages of 6 and 8 Heather developed extreme fears about leaving home overnight without me. I agonized over the past. Was it the bus ride? The episodes were years before, but the guilt was as sharp as if her school bus were still rounding the corner twice a week.

I write about these happenings now because, irrational as it may be, I'm not entirely over the guilt. I still wake up in the night and think of these and other incidents. I would like to stop. Guilt is a useful tool if it hits one immediately and can be used as a mobilizing force to change a current circumstance. Yet guilt can be a negative, self-deprecating blinder on one's creativity when it goes on for years.

Many parents I have talked to have struggled with similar guilt issues. One young woman I knew years ago set a good example when she admitted, "I now *own* the fact that I may have damaged my two boys by staying in a destructive marriage too long. Now that I own that fact and have stopped agonizing over it, I'm a better mom today."

Fathers are just as likely to suffer from parental guilt and anger as mothers, comments family relations authority Joseph Procaccini in a *U.S. News and World Report* article this month. Men are less likely to talk about it, however.

Two years ago I discussed the sometimes crippling effect of parental guilt with a sensitive older friend. When, in speaking of my early child-rearing years, I said, "I tried to do the best I could, but"—she interrupted me kindly and said: "You don't do the best you can. You do the best you know how—the best you know how at the time. Just because you

learn more later, you shouldn't blame yourself for not knowing it then. And sometimes things don't work out for every
member of the family, even when you're doing the best you
know how."

In the August 1982 edition of *Ms.* magazine, author Gabrielle Burton illuminated my friend's advice: "I was guilty all
the time; that made me mad, too. It took a long time for me
to give myself permission to work and to parent. To do my
best and not feel one hand was robbing the other." Speaking
of the relationship between herself and her husband, she
wrote, "Looking back, I think we grew too isolated, turned
to one another too much. But we were doing the best we
knew how."

Arthur Gordon, in an essay called "The Secret of Self
Renewal," tells of advice he received from a Denver
psychiatrist. "Step out of your own shadow," said the
psychiatrist. "Stop judging yourself so harshly. . . . Stop
focusing on your shortcomings and give yourself credit for a
few virtues now and then. . . . People need to be kinder to
themselves because very often self kindness reduces the
feelings of guilt and inferiority that are blocking the flow of
power from the unconscious."

And when that power is released from the unconscious,
perhaps "the best we know how" may indeed become "the
very best we can," even in child rearing.

March 21, 1983

Not Just for the Babies, But for You

As I sit at my desk and review a particularly rich encounter with my daughter this morning before she left for
school, I feel a certain sadness, vague in its origin but strong
in its impact.

What is wrong? What is sad? Is it the present? No. She is
developing well and on schedule. Our relationship, though
charged with the inevitable clashes of a middle-aged mother

and a budding adolescent female child, is strong, vital. We are bonded.

Is it the future? Do I mourn in advance the time she will leave home and our rich encounters as well as our battles will be fewer? No. Much as I love my children, I do not fear the empty nest. Nor do I dread the loss of my active "mother-self." My person-self, my writer-self, my wife-self already envisions the new multi-dimensional leaves and buds which will sprout from the tired but flexible twigs of the vacant nest.

It's not the present or the future, but the past which reaches up and pulls on my "mother-strings." This sadness for the past is not streaked with guilt. It's not a worry about whether I chose the right nursery school, disciplined the children for the wrong things, didn't discipline them for needed things, lost my patience too often, twice forgot to alert the tooth fairy, etc., etc. Parental guilt I have given up, totally—well, almost.

This sadness comes not from any past action but from my past attitude. During my 15 years parenting, I have done many other things. I still do those other things, some with full energy, others with feet dragging. Yet as I do them, I realize that parenting is the single most important and also the most fulfilling thing that I do. I know that, now.

I may have known it even then—then being the baby years. But I did not receive the validation I needed to acknowledge my knowledge. My relating with my toddlers was tinged with, "This is great, but it isn't enough. I must do something else to justify my existence." Incessant head chatter—all the time—about making a mark on the "real" world.

"I'm a homemaker" didn't cut it in the circles in which I moved. My female colleagues at my part-time job were paid for 40 hours but they worked 60. None was married. None had children. The males I associated with politically and socially thought they were liberated but really were patronizing. One called me "mother" from the time my first pregnancy began to show. To him, my bulging stomach seemed to signal the death of my brain.

Though men gave lip service to the "importance of motherhood," their real measure of personal worth was the dollar made or the cause championed. Feminist friends, though convinced they were marking their departure from the "male mentality," said essentially the same thing: Satisfaction and impact is not found with the ABC's of home-based child nurturing, but within the four P's of outside progress: politics, professionalism, promotion and pay.

I am not sad that I worked outside the home. What saddens me is that I did not come home from my job with my mind and heart open only to the children. That when I did terminate my paid employment, I was compelled to rush around finding "meaningful outside projects." That I seldom felt the full joy of parent-child interchange, because even when my hands did their soothing, my arms did their hugging, and my lips did their story-telling, my head was off elsewhere—in the "real" world.

Author Linda Burton writes about trying to hire quality child care for her infant children and finally deciding to stay home herself for a while: "Slowly, painfully, after really thinking about what I really wanted for my children and re-writing advertisement after advertisement, I came to the stunning realization that the person I was looking for was right under my nose. I had been desperately trying to hire me."

Well, after my daughter was born, I hired me, but I didn't pay myself well enough. I didn't give myself enough strokes. I didn't give myself the mental freedom to enjoy the satisfaction of the real world of my kids.

This confession is not the prologue to an old-fashioned plea for all mothers to stay at home full-time with their children. In this economy it's clear that most mothers can't. And many mothers shouldn't. Instead, it's a new-fashioned challenge to both mothers and fathers with jobs, careers, or other demanding outside interests.

Go ahead, work for pay. Work for satisfaction. Work for fun. Work for strokes. But when you're done, leave the work at the office, the factory, the school. Come home and be Mom. Come home and be Dad. And if either of you can afford it, take a leave of absence and stay home for a period in the "baby" years—not just for the babies, but for you!

April 18, 1983

Poignant Memories of Halloweens Past

October 31, 1980.

I jog by my daughter's elementary school and see the mothers and a few dads waiting on the benches by the tree. What did I forget, I think. Did my fourth-grader not tell me? Should I be there?

Halloween! I remember with a sudden start. The brilliant sunlight has eclipsed my Halloween remembrances. Never in all my Halloween days as a primary grade mother would the weather have dawned this clear. I forgot it was Halloween because the sunshine doesn't fit the chilling, clammy memories of Halloweens past. Seven years of observing the "K through 3" costume parade circle the damp cement school yard. Seven years of stamping feet against the cold and chattering with other mothers to pass the time. Seven years of watching kitties, bunnies, goblins, witches, Darth Vaders, and Snow Whites grasp at their hats and trip over their too-long trousers or tails—and wondering if pneumonia would strike us all dead by tomorow.

On occasional years—usually a busy election year—one child would invariably ask, "Can I go as a haunted house or as a giant pumpkin? John's mother made him into a house last year and it only took her two days!"

On non-election years, smiling and guiltily solicitous, I would ask way ahead, "What exciting halloween costume can we make you this year?"

"You make? Naaah! I don't want to be different—let's just go to Woolworths and buy a skeleton."

Halloween. Not my favorite holiday. Halloween. So much enervation and preparation for such short-lived joys. Halloween. A commercial hype designed to keep the candy manufacturers and dentists in business during the lull before Christmas.

I'm ten minutes past the school by now. Maybe if I turn around and go back I'll catch the end of the costume parade. I quicken my step, relieved that the way back is slightly downhill. Maybe.

The school is a block away. Parents cross the street, wave to each other and get into their cars. The yellow and brown leaves whisk around the deserted sunstreaked playground as a flash of white indicates the last little ghost has entered the lunchroom door.

A lump arises in my throat and I suddenly think of my mother-in-law. A few years back she had seen a group of parents lined up for a spring spaghetti supper at a new elementary school. "Let's go," she had said to my father-in-law. "He looked at me as if I suddenly had gone plumb crazy," she confided to me later, not noticing I was looking at her in the same way. "I just wanted to look at the kids and feel like my kids were little again," she explained. "So we went and were welcomed. Everyone thought we were someone else's grandparents."

The lump stays in my throat. My kids also will not be little again. After seven years of grudging goodwill, now past that stage of Halloween forever, I had really wanted to see that little parade.

October 26, 1981

VI: Home Is Where the Heart Is

For all those with extended families, rich childhood memories, and a house of their own to maintain—

. . . I cannot wish I had been nurtured in a different place. It was the only garden I knew.

Susan Allen Toth

Home Is Where Heart Is Full of Special Meaning

As I deplane and wave eagerly to my mother, reality hits me with full force. This is the last time I'll be going home to the white stucco house in which I grew up, to the wood-ceiling residence in Palo Alto that has been in the family for 34 years.

As a flight attendant, I flew home many times, but home then was not thought of as special. Except perhaps for the traditional Christmas and Easter holidays, home was simply a place to ravish a deliciously prepared meal before rushing off to rendezvous with high school and college friends. But today I don't think of those friends; many, in fact, I can scarcely remember. I think, instead, of my father.

"I always wish you could stay longer," he said once at the airport concourse. He spoke with a rare show of vulnerable demonstrativeness, unlaced with his usual protective humor.

"So do I," I responded unabashedly—for the first time realizing that home was where my parents were. And now, years later, but still too soon, my mother will sell the house.

It was August 1946 when the old gray Chevy rolled its way

westward across the country, my father at the wheel. Our family sang jubilantly, played "cemetery," and counted the license plates representative of different states to pass the time.

Yet, snuggling down in a new motel each night, I had muffled my sobs in my pillow while everyone else slept. I was leaving my best friend. Would I ever make another? Even a dog, which I had been promised when we got into a "real house," wouldn't make up for missing Linda.

My mother and father were following their dream. My sister, Jane, was too young to care. "Goodbye, stupid!" she had said to New York City, as my father had urged us to "take one more look at the George Washington bridge."

"Don't say that!" I had whispered at her fiercely, fighting tears and a huge ache in my throat.

Jane and I slept on army cots in a state of terror our first night at the new house in 1946. Not only did the floors creak, but our father had just told us about the San Andreas fault and the San Francisco earthquake of 1906.

"Will it happen again?" we asked, wide-eyed.

He drew on his cigar. "It might," he said reflectively, "but don't worry. It's still better than living in New York."

Really? Terror stricken, we lay stiff, sleepless, in the dark—waiting for the first tremor of the end of the world.

Today, I read and write in the same bedroom where we had set up the camp cots. Twenty years later the room welcomed the new generation, a crib in the corner announcing the arrival of grandchildren. At that time, home indeed became special—my once-a-summer week of refuge from responsibility when my first child was small.

Now, hearing the shrieks of teenagers, I glance out the window. In faded Levis and multi-colored backpacks, both boys and girls are cycling by on their way home from junior high. So free, so different from us walking with mincing steps in our white "bucks," each movement constrained by our near-ankle-length, tight skirts. Back in the 1950s. . . .

Suddenly, I'm engulfed by memories of those early morn-

ings 10 years ago, mornings of awakening, knowing something was wrong, but not remembering what. Mornings
when the silence screamed.

My father's foot was no longer on the stair; the gentle,
adroit engineer's hands did not open the closet door to
retrieve the red plaid jacket which he would wear when he
rode his bike to work. The key did not turn in the floor
furnace as it used to, taking the chill off the downstairs for
Jane and me. Then, slowly, would come the sick realization
that those particular sounds would never be heard again.

My last day at home I haltingly cull 250 of my father's best
Kodachrome slides from a total of more than 2,000. At first I
feel guilty and almost nauseated by the light click of sound as
a discarded slide hits the metal wastepaper basket. He was a
photographic perfectionist. How do I pick the best shot of 10
winter white scenes of Yosemite Falls? Which view from the
high mountain trail between Lake Tahoe and Echo Lake
best captures the rapture and surprise of each family hike?

Yet, slowly, the task becomes liberating; a sense of power
surges forth. In some way, through this process, I can select
my memories: all those hydro-electric dams we drove over
rugged, dusty roads to examine, protesting with each bump,
"We'd rather play at the beach!"—gone with a toss to the
basket. Jane's third-grade birthday party where I, the
gangly preadolescent ugly duckling, tower over the little
princess—gone with a flick of the wrist. I choose a combina-
tion of my father's best art and my best memories: what a
rare opportunity to reorder the past!

The next day as my mother and I back out the driveway
and head toward the airport, I don't look back. "You can't
take it with you!" my father used to say. I pat my box of 250
perfectly arranged slides and smile. Maybe I can. Maybe I
can.

December 8, 1980

Thanks Is Best Given While the Recipient Can Still Appreciate It

My mother is not dying. True, she will have minor exploratory surgery tomorrow. The chances are nine to one that, at 73 years of age, she'll recover her normal vigor, her spryness and optimism slowed only by a slight and occasional arthritis of the knees. They why do I write this—the kind of tribute recited usually over the graves of the dead?

I write to remind myself of the lesson I learned 12 years ago:

We didn't really have to call my parents. They understood that the phone lines from Florida to California would be clogged on Christmas Day. Now it was a day later.

My husband and I were sitting on our pile of climbing gear in the Miami airport. The plane for Mexico City, which would connect us with the others who would climb the volcanoes of Mexico, was delayed. Exhausted from the mere preparation for the trip, I argued with myself whether or not to walk the seeming mile of tiled airport concourse and stand in line for the pay phone. One more try, I thought wearily as I forced myself off the rolled-up sleeping bag.

"Hello," said my father.

"Thanks for the articles and maps of the volcanoes—they were great. And a late 'Merry Christmas'!"

"Same to you. Your mother's not here—she'll be sorry she missed your call."

"How are you?"

"Fine—a little pain in my chest," he answered lightly.

"It's just because you miss me!" I teased.

"Well, of course," he laughed heartily. "I should have thought of that!"

For the allotted three minutes, we continued with the light banter and warm well wishes that was our special dialogue of affection. I flew off to Mexico City physically and emotionally lifted by the short conversation. Twenty-four hours later, my 60-year-old, tennis-playing father was dead of a heart attack.

The message reached us in a desolate Mexican village between Popocatepetl and Orizaba. I folded, stunned, into my husband's consoling embrace. My first thought was of my mother. My second thought was of myself: "Thank God I made that phone call!"

My mother is not dying. But I won't wait. I won't wait to make those phone calls, won't wait to write those letters, and won't wait to say "thank yous" that someday could dissipate in the wind or echo off the canyon walls with unresponsive emptiness.

Thank you, Mother, now, for that time when Jane and I were 10 and 7 and you said, "You and your sister are individuals—you don't have to be just alike."

Thank you, for when, in my 15th year, you warned, "When you are in love and things don't work out, you want to die. But don't be so careless crossing streets. If you died you would hurt us terribly. But if you survived a cripple, think how you would hurt yourself."

When I was 24: "We don't care about a fancy church wedding, but when you marry, your Dad and I want to come."

When I was 30 and pregnant: "Of course you can have a baby and a career, too! It's not the Depression; it's the 1960s!"

And also, Mother, thank you for not (and it's the "nots" that I've learned as a parent are the hardest)—thank you for not:

Criticizing my friends and boyfriends;

Disapproving of my cooking and housekeeping (even though yours is still far superior);

Saying "You can't . . . .";

Questioning my life's goals, though they are different from yours;

Living your life through me;

Caring excessively for what the neighbors will think;

Becoming defined by the roles of homemaker, mother, grandmother, widow (although you are all of these, you are so, so much more).

Thank you for you—my mother—my mother who is not dying.

August 31, 1981

A Special Father Who Rejected the Mystique That Sons Are Best

My father, who died in 1969, was the only male in a family of four females: his wife, his mother, my sister, and myself. My sister at age 4 took note of his singular status and announced that as he was the only man among us, she would henceforth call him "man" rather than "daddy." And "man" she called him until her pre-teen years.

Yet, outside of his family, our father's professional world was predominantly male, as were his interests. A civil engineer and college professor all his adult life, he taught "male" subjects to young male students. A track participant in his youth, he later evolved into a mountaineer, a football fan, a cigar smoker, a gun collector, and an avid reader of Robert Service poetry.

I must have been about twelve that day, when, between plays at a Stanford football game, I asked my father if he had hoped for a son. Did he ever wish that either my sister or I had been boys? I began the question boldly, but quickly my courage faltered. I hoped he wouldn't notice that my voice stammered and trailed off at the end.

"No, I don't think so," he said thoughtfully as if the question had never before occurred to him. "Name me one thing a son could do that you girls can't do."

"Well, play football. . . ."

"This isn't a sport that *really* matters," he said. "It's individual skills or the companionship sports, things that will last you all your life that are important."

Yes, like tennis, hiking, mountain climbing, skiing, target shooting, and even high-jumping—all of which he had taught my sister and me to do. As we cheered Stanford on to victory, the warm feeling which engulfed me was not only for the team.

Growing up, I thought my dad was special. But it wasn't until years later, through delving into feminist literature, that I learned just how very special my dad was. He seemed totally unaffected by what has been called by one writer "the historical and cultural preference for sons."

In her autobiography, *Changing*, actress Liv Ullmann writes of her birth near Tokyo: "Mama says she remembers two things. A mouse running across the floor, which she took as a sign of good luck. A nurse bending down and whispering apologetically, 'I'm afraid it's a girl. Would you prefer to inform your husband yourself?' "

Psychiatric nurse and author Angela Barron McBride writes in her book, *Living With Contradictions–A Married Feminist*, of her father's reaction when she phoned to announce the birth of her second daughter: " 'Two girls—well, your husband wasn't any more of a man than I was!'. . . . I hung up the phone. My blood turned to ice water. I felt sorry for myself and even more so for my father. I hadn't realized how much he had wanted a grandson. How much of a disappointment had my birth been?"

"The notion that sons are the only children that matter has scarcely changed much over the centuries," continues McBride. "From Adam to Jacob to Henry VIII to the Shah of Iran, to a woman's own mother and father, sons are special and few daughters ever forget it."

In some cultures there are daughters who don't live to forget it. *Christian Science Monitor* correspondent Takashi Oka writes from mainland China that the recent government pressure for "one child per family" has increased female infanticide in rural areas to a frightening degree: "In Jaingsu Province . . . some [female infants] were left in fields, under bridges, and in public toilets. . . . In one county of Guandong Province, more than 130 cases of female infanticide took place last year."

In the United States we do not murder our infant daughters. Yet studies show that most American parents would prefer a boy as their firstborn. A U.P.I. correspondent from Tokyo reports that within two or three years a chromosome-separating technique developed by Japanese researchers could allow parents to choose the sex of their children with astounding accuracy. Will females thus become a dwindling minority?

We are supposed to be living in a liberated, "postfeminism" era, yet a University of Colorado research project, supervised by Alice I. Baumgartner-Papageorgiou, is not reassuring about the value female children put upon themselves. The reseachers asked 2,000 public school children the question: If you woke up tomorrow morning and discovered that you were of the opposite sex, how would your life be different? Among the results, which overwhelmingly pictured boys as the favored sex, were these two answers: From a sixth grade girl, "If I were a boy my father would be closer, because I'd be the son he'd always wanted"; and from a third grade girl, "If I were a boy, my daddy might have loved me."

Which brings me back to my own father. I never doubted he loved me. Most fathers do love their daughters. But my father's special quality may have been that he never once, directly or indirectly, gave any indication that daughters were not just as lovable, just as capable, and just as valuable as any potential sons.

June 18, 1983

Alas, Vacation's Freedom Is All Too Short

The bird taps on the outside of the window, as I pack my things inside the bedroom. I go to the kitchen to finish up the dishes. Outside the windows over the sink, the bird

awaits. Tap-tap. Tap-tap. He's following me, I think, de-
lightedly. During my week-long visit to my mother's house
he and I have become friends.

My mother is not so entranced. "Darn bird," she says.
"You're even encouraging him, and you should see what he
does to my car!" I protest her annoyance. As I eulogize the
"cuteness" of the bird's personality, I hear the voice of my
9-year-old daughter. In fact, I *feel* like my 9-year-old daughter.

Regression runs rampant each time I come home to the
old family house in California, where I can hang suspended
above the cares of the real world. And besides, the car
doesn't belong to me.

My sister's dog, Emily, barks vehemently at the mailman,
then again at the telephone man, and again at the next-door
neighbor. I remember how irritable I became when my old
German shepherd used to do that. But I merely smile at
Emily. After all, she doesn't belong to me.

"What is the owl-like sound in the early morning?" I asked
my mother.

"It's the doves. Sometimes we have to spray them with
water and make them fly away. They damage the roof."

I'm sad for them and think the roof is not so important. I
remember the time my father had my favorite pine tree cut
down. "Its roots are starting to crack the foundation of the
house," he explained matter-of-factly. I was unappeased.
What was a house foundation compared with "my tree"? But
the house didn't really belong to me.

My mother's next-door neighbor tells us indignantly
about packing for her camping trip. Her children were "just
delighted" to find a mother and three baby mice nested in
one sleeping bag, dirtying and destroying the precious down
fill. I suppress a giggle. I'm older than this mother yet,
somehow, I'm with the kids.

And I laugh uproariously at the newspaper feature story
about the precocious sea otter, Tichuk, who wreaks daily
havoc at the Seattle aquarium. Tichuk has been known to

remove the drain of his 74,000-gallon tank and fill it with
rocks. He has a penchant for pulling loose underwater lights
and cables. He removes nuts and bolts from the windows in
his pen and has even invented his own buoyancy compen-
sator: To keep himself steady while he accomplishes his
"task," he lays a 10-pound rock on his stomach.

I wonder if I would laugh so hard at home. Not only do
neither Tichuk nor the Seattle aquarium belong to me, but
on vacation I seem ready to laugh at anything. Weightless,
"non-responsible," and free of possessions, I realize how
much of my humor and affinity for nature have been sacrificed with my increasing responsibility for kids, pets, and
the ownership of "things."

Back in Colorado, the transformation is complete. Re-
sponsible parent I become once again. No longer child with
mother but now mother with one large house to oversee,
two children, one basset hound, nine gerbils, a guinea pig,
and 50 squirrels who live in the trees and dirty the windows.
"Parent" with a capital "P."

"Can I turn my gerbils loose in the bathroom if I keep the
door shut, and can I build a trough of nuts at an open window
to help the squirrels prepare for winter?" My son blurts out
the questions in rapid fire as I come up the stairs.

"Hmmmm," I reply noncommittally. Darn squirrels
anyway.

As the basset hound greets me with joy and rolls over
whining for his tummy rub, I can only think with dread of
checking the marble floors and the corners of each
bedspread to see if he has finally learned. . . .

Heloise, the guinea pig, twitches her nose at me as she
eyes me warily. I twitch my nose back and do the same. "I'll
clean the cage every day if I can keep her for the school this
summer," my daughter had said. Sure. Except when she's
at camp, visiting grandparents, or otherwise importantly
engaged.

Heloise is adorable, caramel-white, and cuddly. If I don't
learn to appreciate her soft ginger fur this summer, I *know*

I'll adore her when I visit "her" class at school in the fall. By then, she'll no longer belong to me.

July 29, 1980

Life's "Moments" Are Kept in Memories

It's summer in New Hampshire, early 1940s. The sprinkler spins round and round. Absorbing the rays of the morning sun, its spray forms a pale rainbow on the white slats of the garage door. The pebbles of the gravel driveway press hot against my palms, leaving a spattering of indentations which, to my wonderment, fade away. I press again.

Enchanted and wonder-filled, that early morning: the smell of clean, soft earth wafting upward, the sunshine washing my back with a sense of well-being. Summer at my grandparents' home. The dew in the grass would still be cool; I knew that by moving a few yards I could trade the hot pebbles under my hands for the lawn's cool, damp lushness on my feet. I chose. I would do that in a minute.

Choosing, knowing, wondering, well-being—my first conscious memory of the wonderment of the world and a sense of myself as an actor in it. I couldn't have been more than 3 years old.

As an adult I have wondered if my memory of that moment would be any more clearly enhanced with a photograph. I doubt it. A photograph may bring back in vivid detail moments we have half-forgotten, but one's most joyous, spontaneous, euphoric moments that feel like "just yesterday" are more clearly etched on the brain—or perhaps on the soul—by memory alone. "Memory is possession," writes poet Jean Ingelow.

Winter in Colorado, 1967. In a trance, we enter the back door of our new home. The Christmas tree bulbs blink with welcome, and the particles of melting snow outside the picture window dance with the intensity of the noonday sun. No music plays, but the combined blinking and sparkling seem a cacophony of song. I sit on the window bench. Home from the hospital with our firstborn child.

We do have a photograph of that moment, but it does nothing to evoke the intensity of feeling: just a typical young woman in a typical black turtleneck and green miniskirt, smiling at at typical tiny bundle of baby, wrapped in blue.

Winter in California, 1969. The upward-licking flames of the robust fire in the fireplace frame the strands of my mother's gold-silver hair as she hugs me in a farewell at the door. I am crying slightly, but she is not. A week after my father's funeral, her faith, serenity, and warmth glow as intensely as the flames. The shock was before; the real sadness would come later. But that moment is neither; instead, it captures an isolated episode of tenderness, joy and reaffirmation. Memory is possession.

Briefer moments flash into consciousness. I cannot go to the Colorado mountains in the summer without recalling my first sunset drive to South Park on a rare evening when the vast range of mountaintops turned purple simultaneously. Nor can I visit the sea without recalling one special bright noontime when the gulls swooped by the open balcony of the San Francisco Cliffhouse. The gulls, white and sleek as their wings reflected the sun, caught my bread crusts in midair as they dove round and round in a hypnotic circle.

Such moments can be connected with love, romantic and familial, but they do not have to be. Love does not make them, though they often illuminate love. "There is no one and only," writes Anne Morrow Lindbergh, in her immortal *Gift from the Sea*, "there are just one and only moments."

Often such moments are connected to pure solitude. None can be planned, and few come from the Big Events in life. Weddings, promotions, inaugurals, and anniversaries aren't likely generators of pure unadulterated joy. Although they herald personal change and progress, their spontaneity can be killed by obsessiveness with detail; their deepest meaning can be sacrificed to their form, their "noteworthi- ness," or social significance.

From those events, photographs abound; but the genera-
tive origins of such events inevitably lie elsewhere—vivid
but unphotographed—where memory alone is possession.

September 15, 1980

The Sewing Machine:
A Symbol of Domesticity with Results

The *Denver Post*, Oct. 9, 1980: "The Singer Company
said Monday it would phase out production of household
sewing machines at its plant in Elizabeth, N.J."

A Singer representative in Denver assures me that the
phase-out reported by the *New York Times* is at the New
Jersey plant only. Household Singers will continue to be
made, as a *Denver Post* November 7 story reported. I'm
relieved. Even the possibility of a total phase-out brings
nostalgic memories sharply into focus:

I sit at my grandmother's feet while her pre-World War II
Singer whirs and clicks over the soft wool of my new navy
blue winter coat. As I finger the anchor-etched brass buttons which will trim the new coat, my grandmother talks to
herself, to the machine, and even to the material, coaxing it
"around the corner" or through another "fussy spot."

Six years pass. "All girls can do is sit home and sew!" yell
the fifth-grade boys as they fly by on their bicycles. "Nah-
nah. Nah-nah!"

"We do not!" we yell indignantly, as we race to catch up.
"We play baseball. We go to Scouts, just like you guys, so
nah-nah to you."

But we do sit home and sew—for one clandestine day a
week. "The Ten Tiny Tinkers" sewing club meets Mondays.
With cotton bought at 35 cents a yard, we do our best to
make "look-alike" dirndl skirts which come out looking so
unalike that no one ever guesses about our club or teases us
about our strictly domestic endeavors.

Six more years pass. In high school I progress to making

my own plaid slacks and strapless formals. I have outgrown
my grandmother's idea of fashion, but not her sewing tips,
which to this day have kept any complicated pattern from
intimidating me. Each Christmas and every spring, literally
miles of taffeta and net take over my grandmother's small
bedroom under the eaves. I still marvel at her patience.

Another six years fly by. Scarcely settled in Colorado in
1959, my first purchase is a $175 Singer. Considering my
stewardess salary of $290 per month, I am aghast at the debt
I incur. Yet, through the years, the Featherweight has
recovered the $175 over and over again, as each knee-length
"shift," burlap curtain, no-iron tablecloth, long hostess
dress, maternity top, mini-skirt, daishiki, Halloween costume and mother-daughter sundress flows out from under
the presser foot to practical use.

"You really should have a new deluxe table model, with all
the attachments," says my mother-in-law in the early '70s,
hinting that she would be willing to pay a good part of the
expense. I shake my head, sensing an unintended trap. "My
old one is fine for all the time I have to sew, but thanks
anyway." I smile privately, perplexed over my refusal. My
second baby is on its way, and I have just quit my social work
job. Yet I am pulled by the beckoning strings of the women's
movement. Perhaps I secretly fear that a new sewing
machine would epitomize total domesticity.

A fancy new machine would reflect guilt. Its presence
would say: "I cost more than $500, and you now should make
everything: underwear, bathing suits, tailored blouses,
diapers, and down jackets." Help!

"All girls can do is sit home and sew!" The taunt of 25
years ago comes back and nettles me. The sewing machine:
the ultimate symbol of female role-designated domesticity.
Possibly. Yet I am pleased when a pro-ERA article I have
written for the *Rocky Mountain News* in early 1978 is accompanied by a pen and ink drawing of a long-skirted,
19th-century woman working her push-pedal machine.
Maybe, I think, the picture will attract some readers who

would be put off by a pictorial accompaniment of "professional" women or placard-carrying marchers.

This weekend, on the old Featherweight, I make a bright red velour ice-skating skirt for my daughter, complete with button and buttonhole. The most tangible accomplishment of the week, I reflect, as I shake out the little skirt and clip it to the hanger.

And that tangibility may be the appeal of sewing, or other stitchery, over most domestic projects. Unlike dishes and floors, which are never really done, and culinary creations, which are devoured before finished, the sewn item stands complete in itself.

November 17, 1980

Christmas: Expectations and Disappointments

A 4-year-old boy cries as if his heart would break. Santa Claus did not bring the hoped-for five-foot fire truck, complete with its own hose and water tank. Suddenly, he stops "mid-wail" and surveys the Christmas scene. His eyes light up. The electric train and the two-foot Teddy Bear look OK! Tears drying, he approaches the latter eagerly, forgetting what he didn't get and avidly embracing what he did.

Christmas expectations: they were sky high when we were young. As children, we were the embodiment of Christmas magic. We glowed with the joy, the sense of rebirth, the relief from routine that the adult-created Christmas season provided for us. Our expectations were high, but so was our flexibility level; we still retained that childhood ability to adjust.

Christmas expectations: we all remember that certain age when we lay awake on Christmas Eve, perplexed and depressed. We were not sleepless out of Christmas excitement, but out of a sense of loss. This year it didn't seem all that important that we receive that pair of skis or that cashmere sweater. We were growing up and our expectations were not as magical; thus, Christmas itself lost some of its magic.

Christmas expectations: it seems we only grow up for a little while. A certain age approaches, perhaps, when we become parents or grandparents and we long for re-creation of the magic. Thank heaven! If none of us reached this stage, who would pass on to the young the joy of giving and receiving the Christmas season teaches us so well?

Yet, in our eagerness to re-create the magic, we sometimes deny the spirit and concentrate too heavily on the specifics. Christmas will be just as it once was as long as Helen and her family come home, the perfectly symmetrical eight-foot tree is decorated in silver and white, and some family member has remembered our oft-repeated hint for the quilted paisley robe in a size 12 with matching slippers.

In one home on Christmas eve, an eldest son arrives unannounced, bringing his new girlfriend and a huge box of hand-made Christmas ornaments for an already decorated tree. "Surprise!" he cries, as he grins boyishly and flings open the door. His brothers and sisters scream and scramble and gather around him.

"My son has disrupted everything!" his mother complains later at a party.

"At least he came home," muses a friend whose children are far away.

In another home, a college sophomore unthinkingly tells a mildly anti-religious joke at Christmas dinner. Her aunt leaves the table in a hurt rage. "You have ruined my Christmas," she sniffs, and secludes herself in her room.

Christmas expectations: longing to re-create the magic of our childhood, we hitch our hopes on what we will get, or how other people will perform. We long to be given to by our loved ones, but when our needs become too specific, we cripple their spontaneity and their willingness to give.

As we grow older we regain the magical expectations of the child within us. But, unlike the child, we have lost some flexibility. We are less likely to be satisfied with the teddy bear when we didn't get the truck. We want what we want, the way we want it, and why can't our loved ones deliver!

A friend of mine in her early 40s called me last Christmas night. She was furious. Her baby daughter, a first child, had celebrated her first birthday along with Christmas. My friend's father, instead of sending a life-size doll, or a bouncy multi-colored ball, had sent a package of dull but practical winter baby clothes. How could he have let her down with such mundane gifts?

A week later she called back and reflected on her reaction. "How dumb I was," she said, "to let my expectations ruin a wonderful Christmas. Mandy is too young to care; besides, who am I to tell my father how to love?"

December 17, 1979

Making Christmas a Family Celebration

It was just the four of us last year for Christmas. Four of us in a great big house. Christmas Eve we sat by the fire and read selections from the *Denver Post* Youth Writing Contest.

"Grandpa was always the first to come out on Christmas morning, in his T-shirt and trousers, with the few hairs on his head scattered wildly, and his teeth freshly inserted," wrote Mary Beth Bonacci, in a fond remembrance of her grandfather's enthusiasm at Christmas time. Our son interrupted, "Why aren't our grandparents here? Why don't we ever have a big family Christmas?"

Ever? My neck stiffened in defensiveness, for the children's grandparents and for us. Ever? Why, we've had "hundreds" of big family Christmases. But the kids were right. For the past few years we had stopped for a myriad of practical reasons.

"It's too cold," said our Florida grandparents, "it's so much nicer to visit in the spring."

"I really prefer Thanksgiving," said our California grand-mother.

"We're just too busy at that time of year," said our New Mexico aunt and uncle who were busy developing their own shopping center.

Yes, practical reasons. But pleasurable and self-centered reasons of our own also. One time we had wanted to go scuba diving, another season we had been offered a house at a ski area for our private use. How could we refuse? And somehow the big family Christmas faded out.

Poignant memories of earlier Christmases washed over me. There were so many when the kids were little. "Don't you remember the 'dollhouse' Christmas, Heather? And the 'Star Wars' Christmas? Everyone was here then. Don't you remember the year Grandma Dot was not only here for Christmas but your birthday, Scott? Don't you remember the year Aunt Barbara sat down to dinner and the chairback snapped off? The year that Uncle Terry brought the merry-go-round horse?"

The kids' faces were blank. "I only remember that they used to come and that they don't come anymore," said our daughter. "Why?"

We were all silent, lonely, lost in thought. . . . I had my part in letting the tradition die. Quickly I realized the reason for the prick of defensiveness: I got tired. Tired of the shopping, tired of the preparing, tired of wrapping not only the gifts I had bought, but other people's gifts for other people, tired of the "piggy" attitude of small children when so many people are indulging them. Tired of generation-gap squabbles. Tired of people in general, after the mansion entertaining season. Tired. . . .

"Santa Claus is a woman!" I muttered resentfully at 2 a.m. one Christmas Eve while finishing the touches for the "per-fect" Christmas. A perfect Christmas—a self-imposed goal, but real nonetheless. Bitterness followed by guilt for feeling bitter.

I never pulled off the "perfect" Christmas, but they were fun, happy, rollicking Christmases nonetheless— emotionally draining, but times when I thought Christmas traditions were being passed on. And yet, our two children can hardly remember! Maybe there was a time to let the big Christmases go, but now, now was the time to aggressively reinstate them.

"Hey," I said, "let's stop moping and let's enjoy each other this year and next year we'll get everybody here."

"Everybody?" said the kids.

"Well, we'll try," said I.

"We'll insist!" said their Dad.

"We'll all go shopping together in Larimer Square," said Heather.

"And we'll all draw names for stockings, and I want to buy the presents with my own money," said Scott.

And this year they are all coming. And I can't wait. And the kids' enthusiasm tells me that it will be they who will be up until 2 a.m. arranging things—and they will do it with more Christmas spirit than I did. (Being younger and smarter, they won't insist on perfection.) And there will be conflicts and an occasional hurt feeling—but that's okay. And we will all be together again. And it's time, it's time.

Our family thanks Mary Beth Bonacci for motivating our family instincts with her gentle reminder in the closing paragraph of her article: "I feel a tear come to my eye every time I see that little man step out in his half-awake state to view the Christmas scene and watch my younger siblings act out my role in that play. I wonder how many more years there will be before this, as the other remnants of my childhood, will pass into memory. And I will savor each and every minute with them, for each Christmas could be the last."

December 21, 1981

Does Tradition Bind at Christmas?

I feel Christmas closing in around me. Concentration on any other undertaking is interrupted by holly-gilded thoughts that float in, get pushed away, only to float back again.

What can I get my nephew? Will the packages to the grandparents reach them on time? Is there anything we can get the children that doesn't send video game "zap-zaps" or hard rock electronic chords ricocheting through four floors? Thank heaven "Pink Floyd—The Wall" now will be replaced by traditional Christmas carols on the stereo.

In many ways our children are more traditional than we are. At ages 12 and 15, they want carols at Christmastime, even in place of Pink Floyd. The big tree that we decorate must be done just so; new ornaments are looked at askance. The tiny brass sleds with their engraved names, given to the children when babies, must shine visibly from the front branches. The miniature tree made of pine cones and the ceramic doves have to be placed precisely on the same shelf as last year; each person's stocking hung in the exact designated spot on the fireplace screen. . . .

As the evergreen scent from the formally decorated first floor fills the upstairs of the house, warm memories of last Christmas descend on me, recreating the joyousness of a huge family reunion. Last December at this time I wrote a column anticipating the arrival of relatives: "And this year they are all coming. And I can't wait. . . ."

And they did come, to a traditional old-fashioned Christmas in a big old-fashioned house. We sang carols on Christmas Eve, accompanied by Heather on the piano. We drew names to decide who would fill whose stocking. We recorded on our tape recorder the grandparents' memories of Christmases of old. We dressed up for Christmas dinner, feeling warm and fortunate for the gift of life and the love of each other.

But this year will be different. Last summer, inspired by a

recent school-sponsored train trip with Heather, my husband suggested a collective family Christmas present to
each other—an Amtrak trip to California. The children
agreed enthusiastically, and soon we will depart from Union
Station for San Francisco to spend the holiday in the Pacific
Heights home of friends who will be skiing in Colorado. Gift
certificates will be left for friends and relatives, and we will
do the last-minute "stocking" shopping when we reach our
destination.

"It just doesn't feel like Christmas," says Heather wistfully as she glances at the ornaments in the storage room still
packed in tissue.

"No, it doesn't, but it will when we get there," I answer.

She is still young, too young to know that tradition,
though it uplifts our spirits and significantly structures our
lives, does not have to bind. Neither does tradition need to
be forsaken for new adventure. As the pioneer families of a
century ago hauled their lace tablecloths and fine china to
the West, we will carry our traditions with us.

We will decorate a tree that our host family is leaving us,
taking with us the little brass sleds. We'll hang our stockings
on the mantle and buy our stocking stuffers in Chinatown.
We'll sing carols, whether or not there is a piano.

Both children, who were thrilled by the idea of a trip in
the sun of last summer, stare longingly at the mountains
capped with snow. "How much skiing am I going to miss?"
demands Scott. But I am excited. Among the gently interrupting Christmas thoughts invading my consciousness is
the long, drawn-out whistle of a train.

I sympathize with our children's recalcitrance. As a child,
I loved my Christmases at home; the Christmases which
rooted me in the traditions I now pass on. I empathize with
their reluctance to travel. Yet I know that the excitement of
the trip will slowly, gradually turn the mental tide, that
when they hear that train whistle their hearts will race like
mine.

This year they will rejoice in our Christmas away. And

next Christmas they will rejoice that we again are at home. And so will I.

December 20, 1982

Home "Angels" Find Ways to Manage

"How do you manage?"

It's been more than five years since we moved into the luxurious 25-room, 9-bathroom, Colorado Executive Residence, and they still are asking "the question." How do I manage the house, the entertaining, the politics, the kids, the career?

Where were they all those years before? Nobody asked me how I managed during the years I worked political precincts in the mornings with a baby on my back, went to my part-time social work job in the afternoon, and arrived home five minutes before the guests came for dinner.

Where were the questioners with the big question when the second child arrived, and the career was shelved for a while? No one was curious or surprised when somehow I managed to wipe two noses, at least a million tears, and cook four meals a day with the left hand, while the right hand cradled a phone receiver literally vibrating with the incessant rumble of constituent crises, legal complaints, and political requests, urgent messages for the husband-father-lawyer-legislator who might not be home in time to return the calls.

Does anyone ever ask a woman "the question" when she needs it to be asked? When she would love to have someone to listen and laud her organizational talents, her energy, and to cry with her over her failures? Did anyone ever ask author Gail Sheehy how she managed before she was well known, back when she was just beginning? Back when, as she herself relates, "the greatest portion of my salary wasn't enough to motivate my surrogate at home to walk down four flights of stairs and buy milk instead of sloshing the baby cereal with Tropicana." No one asked writer Tillie Olsen, during the 20 years she wrote nothing while single-handedly raising four children and working at "everyday jobs" to support them, how *she* managed.

Does anyone ever ask a woman who needs to work how she manages? It seems that the 80 percent of women who work in blue collar, factory, or retail sales jobs are just expected to "manage," period.

Most women do not have a "wife" or another supportive live-in creature. Virginia Woolf calls this supportive creature "the angel in the house, who must charm, sympathize, conciliate . . . be extremely sensitive to the needs and moods and wishes of others before her own," in addition to the normal physical tasks and the management detail that a house demands.

Most women do not have that "angel" in their house. Most women, in fact, *are* that angel in their house; and if they have financial or creative needs, they "manage" to work them in. And, after weeks or months of muddling through, some do so deftly. Says writer Gabrielle Burton, "The children, the mundane tasks have a flip side. All the small ropes binding me are knotted securely; there is no room for slack. If precipices beckon, they must do so during school hours."

Columnist Ellen Goodman writes, "In years of watching working mothers, I've also seen women who move on to a whole new plane of efficiency. Pressure cuts through the non-essentials like a sharp pendulum."

How do I manage? It's simple. In "my" 25-room, 9-bathroom house there is not one angel, but four: an administrative secretary, a cook, and two domestic workers. Without these "angels" I imagine myself prowling the marble floors in curlers and bedroom slippers, cushioning the old red kitchen phone between chin and shoulder. With the free arm, I alternately wet-mop the marble and dry-polish the antiques, never even emerging from my bathrobe except to attend an occasional school conference.

You see, I don't manage. *We* manage. All five of us. So for a good story, a poignant story, ask another woman, one who is still her own "angel"—one who would welcome the chance to talk.

May 5, 1980

"Wee-Bitties" That Block Women's Visions

In one hour, on this late October evening, a delegation of Chinese governors, each accompanied by his entourage, will be arriving for a "state dinner." Downstairs, the mansion employees are busily and efficiently doing what they think they ought to be doing for the occasion. Upstairs, the children and their friends are kidding and jostling each other with a vehemence no more vicious than usual. The combined sounds blend into the characteristic late afternoon "hum" of the Colorado Executive Residence.

But the Gestalt, the total picture, is slightly off. Suddenly, my mind clicks off a series of things that will need to be double-checked: The Chinese are comparatively short. Are the table center pieces too high? Have our American guests been advised of the importance of promptness? Tea will have to be offered as well as coffee—do we have enough? The children will have to be really good; in fact, quiet. The five o'clock darkness is descending, yet their young friends show no signs of heading homeward.

As another list of small items falls into the trouble column of my brain, my ears echo a slow, nagging *déjà vu*. Immediately the nature of the vague chaos registers: preparations are proceeding for a "normal" night of entertaining. This, however, is not to be a "normal" party; and I, the only one conscious of this deviation from "normality," have been too caught up in the outer world demands of the 1980 election to communicate a different set of expectations to staff and family.

Somehow, as if in a dream, I also see myself in the process of seeing. Is it "womanly intuition" or simply the long-term on-the-job training that gives homemakers the power and the burden of seeing the little gaps—the skill of knowing in advance where the comfort level might not come up to par? What gives us, and sometimes us alone, the instinct to spot and correct a few tiny potential trouble spots that in themselves would be noticed by no one yet in their totality could ruin a successful state dinner, or even bode ill for a potentially joyous evening with friends?

Columnist Ellen Goodman writes of how many a wife "would like to take just half the details that clog her mind like grit in a pore, and hand them over to another manager."

Yes, yes, I say, I am that wife. I am that person. And right now at least I'm lucky enough to have numerous managers. Yet, perhaps she misses another crucial point. How does one hand over to another manager the things one alone can see: the "wee-bitty" items that are needed for "this" when a whole other set of "wee-bitties" will be needed for "that"? How does one hand over the gift and the curse of that double vision accumulated over the years—the double vision or schizoid view, which, while allowing occasional flights to the stars, simultaneously keeps at least one foot firmly ensnared in the earthly web of everyday needs?

One doesn't. One can hand over specific jobs. One can back off temporarily, dramatically covering the eyes of one's double vision while hoping for the best. One can stay eternally anchored in detail, thus guaranteeing no slip-ups in hospitality—but never having the "mind stretch" and /or time to do much else. Or one can forge a bumper course somewhere through the middle ground, deciding which "wee-bitties" one will handle and which one will ignore.

But ignoring demands a price. Because often the same family member or intimate friend who will wonder why a woman, especially a homemaker, is so compulsive over "non-necessary" details and will chide her to "forget all that" and to actualize her own goals, might be the first to help when the detail important to him/her has not been attended to. So out of "natural" instinct, fear of criticism, good heartedness, or all three, we stay in tune with the needs of the few and often the many.

The supposed explanations of why more women don't "make it" to the very top of their chosen professions are way off base. "Women are afraid of success": a dated and unproved concept. "Women only work until they get pregnant": a theory devastated by statistics. "Women are physically weaker." All these perceptions are spurious.

Perhaps it's not what a woman is that can block her way to the very top of her field. Her blockage, instead, might come from the myriad web of "wee-bitties" which, because of her double vision, she can't or won't give up.

December 1, 1980

Housework—One of the Facts of Life

The two children at the art show pointed excitedly to the painting of a bronzed naked figure prostrate on a bleak, white desert. Their mother hushed them gently; then, instinctively dropping on knees to their level, she answered their questions on death and dying in words that 3- and 4-year-olds could comprehend.

As the young woman began to leave, I complimented her on the manner she had with her children.

"Oh!" she said, "I should be home cleaning my house!"

"Why?" I asked.

She laughed, "I don't know, but. . . ." She shrugged, smiled and left.

Housecleaning. It's probably the least vital part of homemaking a mother does. But it is with us even when we are gone from the house. I remember housecleaning extremes from my childhood. I was a 7-year-old in a New York apartment. The mother of the little boy upstairs *never* cleaned her house. She was an artist; there were beautiful paintings everywhere. And dirt! Even I, with a 7-year-old's tolerance for disorder, was appalled.

At the opposite extreme was the mother of a fourth-grade girlfriend of mine in California. She never did anything but clean. Every time I was there she was scrubbing: the windows, the sink, the bathroom, the woodwork. When I would spend the night with my friend, her mother would come in to check that our feet were clean enough to climb between her freshly laundered sheets.

These are the extremes, and they should not be dwelt upon. Yet, to some degree, housekeeping is an emotional issue with almost every woman who manages a home. Women's magazines are resplendent with tips on the subject. Many of the hints are useful, but they subtly reinforce the imperativeness of the task. Television ads promote cleanliness as a value above all values. That should not surprise us—a supercleaner buys twice as much soap as an average cleaner, and the average cleaner twice as much as a noncleaner.

Feminists theorize about the value of housecleaning with appraisals ranging from, "it's trivial" to "it's equal to the most professional job and women should be paid for it!" Both extremes ring in our ears.

Housecleaning. Our mothers, dead or alive, look over our shoulders. As Barbara Ehrenreich suggests in the October issue of *Ms.* magazine, "Our ties to our mothers are knotted with a thousand details of daily life—ironing, 'picking up,' table setting." We may conform or rebel, but we don't forget.

Mother's values. Conflicting feminist theories. Television. And "Heloise." No wonder some women, like the mother at the art show, have difficulty stating their housecleaning "musts" coherently. But many are quite coherent, and here's what they say:

"It needs to be done and I'm the one at home," from a childless homemaker.

"I have to impose some order on my life; it's the only thing I do that is instantly measurable!" from a mother of two preschoolers.

"I hate the work and I hate the mess. When the mess begins to bug me more than the work, I do it!" from a homemaker with school-age children.

"I don't do it. I guess because I don't really know how, " from a secretary with teenagers.

"I do it when I'm intensely trying to avoid something I'd rather do even less," from a divorced mother of teenagers.

"Only when my mother-in-law is coming!" from a mother of four children, ages 2½ to 16.

"When things are falling apart personally, it's the way I begin getting my act together. It's easier to start with the house and slowly work into my own head," from a divorced woman, recently remarried.

"I don't do it, we do it!" from a married lawyer with one child.

"When my father died I thoroughly cleaned and reorganized the house, room-by-room, for two weeks. Normally, I avoid it, but then it was the only thing I wanted to do and the only thing I was capable of doing; it was therapy," from a social worker.

"I do very little during the week. The four of us pitch in and do a two-hour blitz on Saturday morning," from a married schoolteacher with teenage boys.

Housecleaning. It seems we are making progress. Very few women, who were willing to discuss it, blamed anyone or anything outside of themselves for their own mental attitudes. Many revealed that house cleaning was something they had come to terms with, that it was no longer the intense emotional issue it had once been.

In fact, most of them took what one of Barbara Ehrenreich's closing paragraphs indicates is the most sensible feminist approach: "Housework is not trivial, nor is it the domestic analogue of industrial production. . . . Housework is a way we try to control our personal environments, no more, no less."

December 10, 1979

Middle-Age Compulsions

My husband and I are succumbing to middle-age habits. Why? Well, we are 46 and 44, respectively. The other morning he remarked on how important it was for him to have his instant coffee in a special large mug made by the Ute Indians. The huge cup allows him to get through the papers before the need for more coffee interferes. Then the day is allowed to begin. "I'm getting middle-age compulsions," he murmured.

I, too, seem to be layering on certain routines, particularly at night. Whereas I used to dive into bed after setting the alarm, and simply fall into dreamless sleep, I now find myself shuffling around doing minor chores in a set pattern: turn off the big lights, turn on the night lights, set the clock radio at a soothing music station for 6:30, set the alarm across the room at 6:40, fill the coffee pot with water so I can plug it in with one hand as I turn the alarm off with the other. Only after all this routine puttering and shuffling is done can I climb into bed and read my current novel for 15 minutes before I fall asleep.

Even daytime routines have become more regular. I used to jog from the house in a zig-zag pattern, anywhere I felt like, any time of day. Now I follow a specific two-mile route daily. I tell myself that it is because the new puppy I am training to run likes the same pathways. But I don't really believe that.

Whatever happened to my old wayward, sloppy, youthful ways? Do we adults give them up, just as our children adopt them so obviously that we are reminded too painfully of our own youth—without really wanting to go back? As our adolescents find their ways to distance themselves from us, do we need to keep control and distance by imposing little routines of personal order on ourselves?

I remember my father reading *Time* magazine every Thursday evening, smoking his cigar in the same chair. I also remember how irrationally annoyed he seemed to be if

Time didn't arrive till Friday. I remember my mother sitting over her second cup of coffee every night after dinner, when everyone had left the table. It was probably her only moment of solitude from the increasing frenzy of two teenagers, a dog, and a mother-in-law in a small house.

Middle-age habits. . . . But sometimes we deviate. Just this morning my husband came to the kitchen for a second cup of coffee with a normal-sized standard cup in his hand.

"But where's your mug?" I asked, suddenly awake. "You're not leaving me alone in my middle-age compulsions and trying to recapture your youth, are you?"

"No," he replied, staring at the cup in his hand with disbelief. "I just forgot. Guess I'm going from middle age straight to senility!"

January 25, 1982

VII: Life Expanding

For all those people who have asked the question, "Is this all?"—

There is a hunger in Americans today for larger purposes beyond the self.

Betty Friedan

The "Wee-Bitty" Things of Life

According to old Indian folklore, we human beings need both the vision of the eagle and the view of the mouse. To be whole, we must allow our spirit to soar, but we also must pay attention to the significance of the little things, the "wee-bitties" of life.

A brief workshop for women I participated in last October brought this message home. The wee-bitties were what we were asked to recall and cogitate upon. "For a moment, concentrate on some little thing that has happened to you over the past few months," said the leader. "Let the big things—marriage, divorce, childbirth, and illness—slide for a while."

Slowly the women responded to the unusual challenge. "The radiant expression on my friend's face when she opened the door to my unexpected visit to her home in another state," said one woman.

"Sitting in the mountains and listening—just listening to the stream," said another.

"How my daughter became 'Mom' to help me keep a week's diet," said a third.

"Watching my daughter feed the seagulls on the ferry boat last summer at Cape Hatteras," I added.

Suddenly, more wee-bitties occurred to me than I could possibly share with the group. My mind tumbled and swirled with small and happy remembrances of the past year: my son saying, "Mom, do you want to play Boggle (my favorite word game) tonight?" when I knew he had more homework than he could manage; the little bouquet of sunflowers in an earthen vase that a special friend brought to me in the hospital.

About a year ago I wrote a column bemoaning the "wee-bitty" cares that beset the American homemaker—the special insights of her own, the "little person" concerns, the creature comforts of others that can keep her glued to the hearth. And it's true, but . . .

No matter how much my "eagle" will soar, no matter how much I delegate wee-bitty items to others, my New Year's prayer this year is that God will keep my "mouse" in tune with the little things which hold their own kernel of relevance, the wee-bitty exchanges and moments which, if not recorded, slip off the side of consciousness forever.

"Take time to smell the flowers," so many of my post-hospitalization get-well-wishers stated in various ways. I am. And I will.

"There is nothing too little for so little a creature as man. It is by studying little things that we attain the great art of having as little misery and as much happiness as possible."

Samuel Johnson

December 28, 1981

"Paradigm Shift": L'il Twist to Reality

The small plastic angular shapes of color form a Christmas wreath at the end of the kaleidoscope. I turn the toy slowly. The red berries grow bigger and cluster together. The pointed holly leaves stretch toward the center along five concentric lines, then retreat to the wholeness of the design.

The wreath itself becomes thicker, then slowly thinner, nearly enfolding itself in the circumference at the rim.

Suddenly the design crashes to the center, reformed into a petaled red rose with symmetrical green spindles thrusting to the edge. The picture is changed completely: the same chips of size and color, yet a totally new pattern.

Marilyn Ferguson, author of *The Aquarian Conspiracy*, uses the example of the child's kaleidoscope when she speaks of the term "paradigm shift." A paradigm is a scheme for understanding and explaining certain aspects of reality. A paradigm shift occurs when a kaleidoscopic change in perception results unexpectedly from the collective weight of minutiae which no longer fit the old paradigm.

A societal paradigm shift can occur when enough people begin to see old evidence in a new way. For example, a different pattern arrangement of the "kaleidoscope chips" of the Vietnam War, first perceived by a societal minority, then finally by the majority, forced all of us to a new paradigm of American power and its limitations. A personal paradigm shift may occur when a person views the same old behavior pattern in someone else but suddenly is struck by the possibility of different motives.

With a flash of insight, a parent may abruptly "see" that his "ornery" toddler's peace-shattering habit of crushing the Christmas tree ornaments into the white carpet isn't just orneriness. The child may do it because he is jealous of his new baby brother, overexcited about his parents' expectations of Christmas, or worried about starting nursery school. The little particles of behavior that heretofore added up to "orneriness" suddenly add up to something else.

An educational paradigm shift can occur when educators in a certain setting begin to pay attention to how people best learn rather than what they should be taught. "I learned never to dwell on a singer's bad habits or mistakes in order to eliminate them," says Jan DeGaetani West, professor of voice at Eastman School of Music in New York. "Instead , I have the singer concentrate on his or her strengths. Sooner or later the mistakes disappear or are incorporated in a new positive whole."

We are presently in a political period when the failure of both "traditional conservatism" and "traditional liberalism" is a cliche on the lips of forecasters and pundits; yet we, the people, have not yet shifted to a new paradigm view of national problems. We laugh at the King in a New Yorker cartoon as he surveys the smashed pieces of Humpty-Dumpty by the wall. "Oh," moans the King, "if I only had more horses and more men!" But by holding tightly to our old problem-solving paradigms like Linus blankets, we, too, show reluctance to embrace an original framework.

Paradigm shifts often originate from the young and the uninitiated, those with no emotional or status investment in established paradigms. Some theorists propose that a paradigm shift can only come as a result of insight, that ultimate "aha!" experience, which cannot be forced ahead of its time. Others are more optimistic. We can consciously and drastically rearrange old minutiae to exciting new to-talities, indicates one theorist: "We simply give our own mental kaleidoscopes a little twist."

December 15, 1980

"Meeting": A Small Word with Big Meaning

"I met someone today." The late Jungian analyst Irene Claremont de Castillejo uses the word "meet" in her writings to interpret a direct and immediately understood human exchange. To paraphrase Castillejo, a true "meeting" is the flowering or the illumination that takes place when two people truly absorb and respond to each other's verbal or nonverbal communication.

"Meeting" in the Castillejo sense can be as brief as a second or as long as a day. True "meeting" can happen suddenly between those who have never met in the conventional manner and perhaps do not even know each other's names. "Meeting" also can occur between those who have known each other forever. I met my sister 40 years ago when she was an infant of 10 days, but we do not always "meet" as we did today over a spur of the moment lunch.

One sign that we have "met" someone is that we are energized rather than exhausted by the communication. Castillejo, in fact, attributes social or relationship fatigue to the degree with which we are not willing to "meet" or be "met" in our daily interchange. "We are only exhausted when talking to other people if we don't meet them, when both of us are hiding behind screens." Souls meet souls; but roles do not meet roles.

Anne Morrow Lindbergh in *Gift from the Sea* says, "I find I am shedding hypocrisy in human relationships. What a rest that will be!" So relieving, so calmly exhilarating, this business of "meeting." One wonders why the spontaneous combustion happens so seldom.

We often don't "meet" each other because we are on different levels of consciousness, suggests Castillejo. Conversely, we sometimes don't "meet" just because we are trying too hard to relate. A relentlessly self-conscious pursuit of the "meaningful relationship" can lead us to ask too many spell-shattering questions, or to over-express our "true" selves in a nonstop verbal barrage. "I asked how he was and he told me," moaned an acquaintance of mine upon returning from lunch with a former business associate.

Another acquaintance, a homemaker without much opportunity to converse with adults, was trying to describe a "charming and brilliant" older gentleman she had suddenly "clicked" with at a dinner party. Her friends kept interrupting as she searched for the right words:

"What was he like?"

"Why was he so charming?"

"What did he say?"

"He didn't say anything," she finally blurted out, laughing. "He listened! Just for a few moments, but he listened!"

Sometimes, we fail to "meet" because we are frightened

of our own realness. For a true "meeting," you must be open and vulnerable, indicates Rajneesh, an Indian spiritual leader. "If you want to meet someone at his center, you will have to allow him to reach your center, also."

January 19, 1981

Creating Each Day Anew Sparks One's Own Creativity

Creativity—we tend to think of it as the unique province of those who wield artists' brushes, writers' pens, or conductors' batons. "Our mother is the creative one; she paints," says a friend of mine in her early 30s.

"I'm not so sure," muses her sister. "Mother dabbles at painting, so she's considered creative. But she's never finished a painting in her life. Dad's the really creative one, building and expanding his own business from which related businesses have sprung. Taking big risks, not being afraid to fail—that's creativity. Dad doesn't paint; but he creates each day of his life anew."

The state of pregnancy is defined by some as the quintessence of creativity. This definition is a male-imposed metaphor, suggests author Erica Jong in a *New Republic* article. To a writer, especially absurd is "the notion that books are like babies, and babies are even remotely like books. For a book's creative demands upon its author end at the moment of publication; while a baby only begins to call forth *conscious* creativity, after it emerges from the unconscious Eden of the womb."

It is not the pregnant woman, but the nurturing mother who is the true creator. As the late California community activist Josephine Duveneck reflects in her autobiography: "Our children's little bodies were so beautiful. I loved to bathe and dress them. Getting ready for bed was often hectic, but tucking them in and goodnight songs and final hugs were so much fun. Even the inevitable glass of water demanded after final bedtime rites was a source of an extra exchange of mutual reassurances. The physical care of their bodies and the nurture of their spirits was a completely absorbing creative vocation."

And the truly creative one is not the passive mother who responds to the "dos" and "don'ts" of the latest child-rearing fad, but the active mother who, like Duveneck, brings her own nuance to each nurturing skill.

Even in post-women's liberation America, many still think of creativity as mainly the province of men. Is this because there are more male artists, musicians, and writers?

Naturally there are, affirms Tillie Olsen in *Silences*. But the former lack of female artistic achievements is due not just to the fact that women have assumed the role of "angel in the house," denying their creativity to smoothe away everyday clutter from the path of male genius. Even more important, quotes Olsen from Elaine Showalter, is the subtle reality that "women are estranged from their own experience and unable to perceive its shape and authenticity. In part because they do not see it mirrored and given resonance in literature. . . . They are expected to identify with masculine experience which is presented as the human one, and have no faith in the validity of their own perceptions or experiences."

But this nonaffirmation, this nonresonance, is changing. Women not only are actualizing their potentials in non-domestic pursuits, but also, because they are seeing their own situations given more validity in female-written modern literature, are beginning to view their domesticities both as creative wellsprings and disciplining structures.

Marilyn Ferguson, author of *The Aquarian Conspiracy*, describes the creative person as the one who is "whole-seeing. Fresh, with child-like perceptions and a sense of flow . . . [the one who can] see what is there rather than what is expected or conditioned."

Creativity is not the sole property of one class. Neither the rich nor the poor, though the poor may have less means to express it. Neither the male nor the female, neither the

172

pregnant nor the unpregnant. Neither the woman who stays home, nor the woman who ventures out. Creativity may be just that characteristic of my young friend's father: the ability and the inclination to "create each day of one's life anew."

January 19, 1981

On Knowing Our Many Selves

The door of our eighth-grade science class flew open and suddenly the school principal was before us. "Ah, science!" he exclaimed, interrupting the teacher and looking—I thought—directly at me. "A basic lesson that you will learn in this class is that each one of you is unique; there is only *one* of you!"

A few years later I worked at a summer camp where all the counselors were to take the names of stars or constellations. I took my own astrological sign, "Gemini," and after a little exploration on the meaning of the term found out that I might not be one but *two*.

Then in college I studied Sigmund Freud with his id, ego, and superego and later Thomas Harris with his child, adult, and parent. By then I was quite convinced that I must, after all, be *three*.

Not so, I learned last summer, when I took a week's course based on the psychosynthesis principles of the Italian psychiatrist Roberto Assagioli. Taught by two men and one woman—a priest, a minister, and a counselor—the course centered around the concept of the "sub-personalities" intrinsic to each person's psyche—not two or three, but eight to a dozen, and perhaps an infinity.

"Let me give you an example," said the counselor to the class. "I have a sub-personality I have named 'Rockefeller.' It is straight, organized, uptight, and boring—but it gets me where I'm going and gets the bills paid on time. I also have a sub-personality called 'Elizabeth.' she is spontaneous, sexual, nonconforming. She loves to make inappropriate comments at restaurants. Then there is 'Little Girl.' She wears patent leather Mary Janes and white socks and is good—so very, very good—so she will be loved. Then there is 'Scholar,' a ruthless intellectual who cares for nothing but things of the mind. And 'Unicorn,' my spiritual, mythical, unique, and solitary beast."

"But you sound like Sybil, the crazy woman with 16 separate personalities!" exclaimed someone from the group. "How can you be so many people and still be sane?"

"Sanity is not sameness," explained the instructor. "I am sane because I know these sub-personalities; I own them, and I make bridges between them. Sanity is not hiding your personalities, but listening to them. Sybil was not crazy because she had so many, but because she couldn't organize them. And we can organize our sub-personalities by choice, once we get to know them."

Thus began five days of internal and spiritual exploration using guided imagery. Led by the instructors in small groups, we were gently prodded to become acquainted with our sub-personalities—to see diads and triads in conflict with each other, to argue with each part, to make friends with each part, to listen to each part. Then we would share our sub-personality dialogues with the group.

According to psychosynthesis theory, sub-personalities do not bother us because they are dark and devious. On the contrary, some are full of light and represent our repression of the sublime. But they can appear bothersome when we exclude them from our consciousness. Like characters in our dreams, they would not appear at all if they were not trying to tell us something.

Some of my own sub-personalities parade before me as I try to complete this column.

First there is "The Judge." He is stern, unforgiving, moral, and moralistic. Then there is "Morgan le Fey" from the play *Camelot*, who lives for nothing but "passionate afternoons, gluttonous nights and slovenly mornings," There is "Scout Leader," my own personal "Rockefeller."

And there's "Jocko," who loves Scarsdale diets and is sure to run a marathon before she's 50.

The minister's voice comes back to me. "We don't have to act out all of these sub-personalities. But we have to listen and choose." I prefer "Morgan le Fey" or "Jocko" on this beautiful fall day. But I'm on deadline! I hear the Scout whistle in the distance. And if I shut it out, I'll choose a stronger tune. It's called, "Here Comes the Judge."

October 19, 1981

Marathon Days Can Take Breath Away

Mara—mara—mara—thon. My head swims with the opening theme of Friday night's performance of *Jacques Brel*. Now, it's Saturday morning "marathon." I've over-slept. At 8:50 a.m., daughter and friend have ice-skating lessons. It's 8:30 and they're still in their nightgowns, happily making orange crush in the new blender.

"Heather, get your feet moving—now!"

Son needs a $4.50 check. Today, before I leave. Never mind for what. He has the cash; he'll pay me later. The dog is barking, needs walk and food. The guinea pig is sick—please, Lord, not another death in the animal family.

"Scott—walk the dog—now!"

The car needs loading. The column needs writing. The Governor's Cup Cross Country Ski Race is in Devil's Thumb Ranch, two hours away. We must be there by 11 a.m.; it is now almost 9:00 a.m.

I'm racing to race to a race. I laugh abruptly. And on my schedule is clearly marked, "Saturday; DAY OFF!"

Mara—mara—mara—thon.

Problem is, I think (as I settle in the back of the car, unapplied makeup, suntan lotion, and comb falling off my lap, unread newspapers from the week falling off the seat) that I've got to get three columns in before leaving next week for the Governor's Conference in Washington, D.C.

Problem is, I cogitate obsessively, two articles are in the making, but none is in the concluding, and one is not even in the beginning. Problem is that when I get into this frenetic, compulsive, up-tight state, I can't see a possible column if it should hit me broadside or magically spring from my granola bowl in the optimal 12 inches of type.

Maybe the six miles of cross-country fresh air will break the downward spiral of the Monday through Friday "marathon," which this week so rudely and inconsiderately threatens to consume Saturday, too. The gun goes off. The race is on. I move slowly, deliberately, taking a deep breath. Their race is on. Mine is finally off—at least for the weekend.

The breeze flows gently from the east, then gusts suddenly from the north. The sun breaks intermittently through high white cirrus clouds, often enough to add sparkle to the crisp day but not so often as to stick one's skis to the snow, or adhere the prickly wool sweater to one's back. The odor of hot spicy chili cooking back at the ranch makes even us non-racing "racers" think of hurrying—a little.

Marathons. How do we get caught up in them? Those wicked, debilitating mental and physical activity cycles which make others say of us, "They can't see the forest for the trees."

Marathons come in different sizes and different intensities, I muse, as I pause to poke a pine tree branch with my ski pole and watch the fine snowdust sift down in the sunlight. When we are caught on a small, narrow, tightly constricted, personal marathon course, perhaps we "can't see the forest for the trees." But when we get caught on the wider, whirling, worldly carousel, isn't it more likely that we "don't see the trees for the forest?"

I poke another branch of the stately symmetrical tree. This weekend I'm not going to miss any "trees," nor the forest either, I resolve. No sooner resolved, than next

week's column is there in front of me, virtually etched
almost word for word in the ski tracks ahead.

Before you cross the street
Take my hand.
Life is what happens to you
While you're busy
Making other plans.

John Lennon to his son Sean

February 23, 1981

Travel Intensifies Things

When one is traveling, the little nuances of personality,
the idiosyncracies of situation heretofore ignored, suddenly
loom with fresh import. Minor things, which merely sim-
mer at home, can precipitously burst into flame on a trip.

First, there's the weather. When one is on the road,
sunshine is no mere good omen for jogging or watching
summer soccer practice, but a poetic experience:

Oh joy! A new year is begun
What happiness to look upon the sun!

William Morris

Conversely, rain, fog, and snow portend disaster when
one arrives at that special place determined to see its joy-
ously anticipated treasures made brilliant by sunlight or
romantic by sweet haze.

Then there's eating. On a trip, the taste buds sharpen; the
cuisine is carefully judged, the tenderness of each morsel
luxuriated over—or disdained. Amounts of food can become
urgently significant.

In 1961, a roommate and I, on a shoestring budget,
traveled through European ski areas staying each night at a
different "bed and breakfast" *pension*. Each morning our
chatter would cease as the bread, croissants, jam and coffee
arrived from the kitchen. Instantly feeling starved, we

would eye each other with suspicious defensiveness. "Whoever cuts the bread, the other chooses the half she wants," became the rule which saved our friendship—a rule usually reserved for the peaceful raising of competitive children. But travel is not a "normal" time, and on our trips we all, in a way, become children.

Dollars on a trip loom larger than life. They are spent foolishly or hoarded needlessly, often on the same day. On our 1963 honeymoon trip to South America, my husband and I agreed we would not go to Lima's famous Trece Monedas restaurant. We could not go! We were budgeted to $1 a day per person for food and the Trece Monedas was exorbitant—$3 per person, including wine and dessert. Yet we bought llama wool sweater-coats at the marketplace for $25 apiece because they were "so distinctive," and we thought someday we would wear them skiing (we haven't).

When one is traveling with another person, irrational breakdowns in communication occur at regular cyclical intervals. Suddenly being together becomes too much, out of sync, out of whack, or out of tune. Miraculously the "crazy days" disappear as quickly as they come, often without the laborious "working out" process needed to solve conflicts at home.

Travel. The very word denotes that we are not as solidly based and practical as when in regular routine, so the highs and lows take over. We are still ourselves, only magnified; more sparkling, yet more fragile.

September 7, 1981

Looking at the Effects of the "Me Decade" Positively

The middle-aged father who deserted his family to ride motorcycles and pursue 18-year-old maidens. The young mother who, with a click of a gate, left husband and pre-schoolers to fend for themselves in suburbia. The young college student who rejected his education to follow the promises of sensitivity training, primal therapy, est, the

Order of Hare Krishna, without so much as a thought of
those parents who made supreme sacrifices for that education. We all know of the extreme examples of the "Me
Decade." But their lives have little to say about the lives of
most of us.

The "Me Decade": the 1970s. Before they slip away
forever, let's look at those years from another perspective.
For rather than a negative reaction resulting from negative
factors, the argument can be made that the "Me Decade"
was a positive withdrawal from positive forces: civil rights,
environmentalism, feminism, consumerism.

Some of the "me-ism" has been simply a coming home
exhausted after an involvement with activism that didn't
deliver fast enough—or delivered so fast that it promoted
conflicting forces which swirled around us in too many directions simultaneously. For many of us "me-ism" was a way of
becoming centered, of temporarily "getting off" the planet.
Possibly it was a healthy taking stock, a way of slowly absorbing future shock in a world where the only constant is
change, most of which we helped bring about ourselves.

Most of us didn't run away or drop out, and if we did, we
usually came back. For most of us "me-ism" has been a way
of wrestling with smaller, formerly neglected problems
which in our own lives can be most traumatic. For "me-ism"
in its best sense is assertiveness, and assertiveness can
exemplify:

The homemaker who, although she earns no money for
the family, begins taking one day off a week, pays a babysitter, and develops her hobbies.

The father who tells his boss, "No, I can't work Saturday
and Sunday and miss my child's birthday weekend."

The college student who doesn't drop out but says to his
parents, "Yes, you did pay for my education, and I'm grateful, but hey, I can't become a lawyer like you want; it's my
life and law just doesn't interest me."

The young child like my daughter, who recently said to
me in tears, "I'm just 9 years old, and I know I have to do

what you say; but you aren't even listening to my feelings and I'm scared."

Perhaps "me-ism" in its positive sense is all the little people of the world learning to say, "Listen to me! I have feelings; I have needs; I have a destiny to pursue and I want to take more control over my own life." "Me-ism" isn't necessarily getting all one wants, but it is knowing what one wants and being less afraid to go after it.

Socrates taught humankind: Know yourselves; and above all, to your own selves be true. Jesus said in Matthew 22:39, "Thou shalt love thy neighbor as thyself" (not better than thyself).

"Me-ism" has been blamed for everything from the falling productivity rate to the increase in child abuse. Yet, modern psychologists have shown repeatedly that a person who doesn't love him/herself is incapable of truly loving others. Child abusers probably haven't had too much "me" in their lives, but too little.

Most people are simply searching for rootedness, a base from which to operate, a concept that psychologist Bob Samples call "Selfness." Selfness, says Samples, allows one to operate from a center of strength. Selfness avoids both the dangerous extremes of selfishness (which can lead to the narrow, dishonest acquisitivenesses of a Watergate) and selflessness (which can become the kind of wild self-abnegation leading 950 people to commit suicide at Jonestown.)

The "Selfness Decade," as a phrase, lacks the pizazz and self-flagellating titillation of the "Me Decade." But maybe we should rename the '70s anyway. And possibly we should view the decade not as a time in which we lost ourselves, but a time in which we examined ourselves, reclaimed ourselves, and taught ourselves to relate more honestly to others, thus building a stronger foundation for activism in the future.

February 4, 1980

Joy at the Existence of Other People

I was eight the year my father and I went to climb the cliffs
of the New Jersey Palisades across the Hudson River from
our apartment in Riverdale, New York. We carried a small
metal camping mirror. At exactly noon we would shine the
mirror back over the Hudson River and my mother and
sister would signal us back with another mirror from the
fourth-floor window of our apartment.

As their tiny mirror twinkled across the miles in the
Hudson haze, my imagination ran wild! Suppose everyone
in every apartment window had shined a mirror? I could
visualize the sultry day lit up in a horizontal stream of stars
along the river. Every apartment window! Think how many
families lived in those apartments thinking their thoughts
and living their lives. And if there were that many families
along the Hudson, how many in New York? In the United
States? In the world?

"What are you daydreaming about?" my father asked as I
stood there staring, even though the twinkle had long since
disappeared.

"Nothing," I said, as I usually did when asked about my
daydreams. Besides, how could I explain my sudden
insight—that I was a part of all people—even people I would
never know, and perhaps wouldn't like, and that this belong-
ing made me feel warm and closer to God than anything I
had ever heard in Sunday School.

The humanity insight. The person awareness—that part
of a whole. The simple joy at the mere existence of other
people. Since that year of my awakening, I've found many
others who share the same awareness. "Ontology" is what
Madeleine L'Engle terms it, as she describes the moment
from her own childhood:

"I was seven or eight years old. We lived in an apartment
on East 82nd Street in New York. My bedroom window
looked out on the court, and I could see into the apartments
across the way. One evening when I was looking out I saw a

woman undressing by her open window. She took off her dress, stretched, stood there in her slip, not moving, not doing anything, just standing there being.

"And that was my moment of awareness; that woman across the court who did not know me, and whom I did not know, was a person. She had thoughts of her own. She *was*. Our lives would never touch. I would never know her name. And, yet, it was she who revealed to me my first glimpse of personhood. "

I find myself experiencing this sense of ontology when I look upon a city from afar; I feel it when I watch a happy family that does not know it is being watched in a restaurant; I sense it on the trails of the Rockies, on the bustling streets of New York, the public school yards of Denver at lunch time.

But there are times when I lose it. Once was in India in 1967. The pavement swelled and seemed to rise with the stifling heat. The beggars, the sellers, the tourists swarmed among the bodies, some sleeping, some sick, that lay on the streets of Calcutta. The suffering was appalling. Every afternoon a shade of weariness lowered my eyelids, and I would almost run back to the hotel room, not having the energy to come out and deal with the "sights" again till the next day.

Aghast at the way the upper caste Indians would simply step over the bodies of the ill and dying, my husband and I were unkind and cutting about those who would approach him as a public official, mistaking him for a congressman, hoping he would find a way for them to emigrate to the United States. Yet, as we extended our stay there, we became more aghast at something else: ourselves. Slowly, we, too, were becoming like the upper caste Indians, stepping over the dying and the ill deftly, swiftly, as we proceeded on our way to view marketplaces and historical monuments.

How quickly we learned to divorce ourselves from their misery. One hungry person is possible to help; a hungry society is beyond individual efforts, and the mind numbs to the enormity of the suffering. The scene was so overwhelming—one had to divorce one's self in order to survive, to stay psychologically intact.

It is this self-protective reaction that comes back to me when I read of the burgeoning populations in undeveloped countries—the 600 million of India, the billion plus in China, the 3 percent a year increase in Latin America. When I hear on the national news that Mexico alone will double from 70 million to 140 million shortly after the year 2000, I worry about the starving poor, the infant mortality rate, and the potential revolution of the "have-nots."

But I worry also about the "haves." All people need counterpoint: a balance between closeness and space to appreciate humanity. The yin and yang of existence is both embracing and standing apart. As crowds increase on any continent, it's not just the bodies of the dying, but the souls of the living that may wither. Once we lose that childlike awe in the mere existence of other people it becomes easier to "step over the bodies." And once we shut our eyes to take that first step, the chasm between compassion and crass disregard yawns irretrievably. Thus, all humanity is threatened.

November 2, 1981

Our Military "Emperors" Are Naked

A couple of years ago my daughter and I had the following conversation:

Heather: Why are we building nuclear bombs?

Mom: I guess because the Russians are.

Heather: But couldn't that mean the end of the world no matter who sets them off?

Mom: Yes.

Heather: Then why don't we just stop?

Mom: It's not that simple. We have to negotiate. . . .

Heather: I don't understand. Why don't we just stop—all of us—the Russians, us, everybody! Why don't we just stop?!

My daughter's outburst reminded me of the child in the parable "The Emperor's New Clothes." The emperor and his court had been duped by the royal tailors into believing that anyone who could not see the nonexistent clothes they had "tailored" was hopelessly stupid. When the emperor paraded through the streets to show off his "finery," it took an innocent child to declare, "But the emperor is naked!"

Children can expose a basic truth with one comment because they have little investment in the established order. For adults to see truth as clearly takes a leap of faith, a letting-go of old mind-sets, a process that historian and philosopher Thomas Kuhn calls "paradigm shift." According to Kuhn (as quoted by Marilyn Ferguson who expands on his thesis in *The Aquarian Conspiracy*), "A paradigm shift is a distinctly new way of thinking about old problems." It is not a gradual process. It occurs all at once. The new paradigm is not "figured out" but suddenly seen.

Children see because they are not encumbered by old paradigms. The child in the parable saw that the emperor was naked because the child's livelihood, prestige, and belief system did not yet count on the emperor presenting himself in a splendorous manner. The child's truth did not depend upon the emperor seeing the truth.

The modern child can see the futility of the nuclear arms race because she or he has not yet been brainwashed by generals who, since the invention of the bow and arrow, have preached that the side with the most weapons wins. The child can see that if one lad has seven matches and the other nine, each is equally capable of burning down a barn filled with hay.

During the Vietnam war, thinking adults began to see the paradox and the hypocrisy of another military paradigm. When military defenders said, "We had to destroy the village to save it," these adults did not nod their heads in a

stupor. Instead they challenged the old mind-set: Destroy?
Save? How are these words possibly compatible?

Just this Christmas a friend sent me a message that was a
new paradigm view of a military invention. The message
began with a headline from the *New York Times* of August 9,
1981: "Reagan orders production of two types of neutron
arms for stockpiling." The newspaper article continued,
"These weapons are designed to produce far more radiation
and far less blast and heat than other tactical nuclear
weapons so that they kill people without severe damage to
their surroundings."

My friend's message ended with a poem she conceived
after pondering the *New York Times* story.

> The house still stands.
> Bookcases along the wall replete with volumes,
> Poetry, music, art, some mysteries, some fiction.
> The desk holds stationery, pens and stamps,
> Unfinished letters, notes reminding someone to pay bills.
> Collect the laundry.
> Get the children shoes for school.
> Outside the garden flowers in the sun.
> Roses and peonies go unpicked,
> Bicycles lean against the wall.
> Tennis racquets sprawl across the court.
> Somewhere the bell of a Good Humor Truck rings idly
> Propelled by the wind, and clocks strike hours.
> A cat, perhaps a dog, a mouse, moves shakily, sniffs for
>   food.
> And listens.

Eugenia Rawls

January 31, 1983

Going For a Walk On a Spring Day

It's a crazy, bright Colorado spring day. One of those gorgeous, clear, still days that sneak in between the hailstorm days and duststorm days, the harsher and more characteristic harbingers of spring near the Rockies. Today is different, a jewel of a day.

A friend drives my son and me to the orthodontist. I decide to walk the four miles home. "I'll pick him up," says my friend, acting as if my midmorning urge on a hectic day is perfectly normal.

On the park lake, ducks squawk, flap their wings, and jostle each other for bread crumbs tossed by equally squealing and energetic children. The reflected sunlight on the water sparkles so intensely that the particles of light seem to explode back to the sun. The earth smells like saltwater, and the Denver lake at 5,000 feet altitude suddenly feels connected to the Cape Cod and Monterey coves of distant coastlines.

Today, the New Year's resolutions go out the window. Ponderous problems begin to solve themselves. Suddenly anything seems possible. The kids might stop fighting over the rocking chair in the television room. The 3-year-old basset hound will be completely housebroken by summer. Women bank presidents will become as common as male telephone operators. The draft won't be necessary for women—or for men.

A few blocks from home, I am stopped by a spry and dignified elderly gentleman on a brisk walk.

"Excuse me, Ma'am, are you married?"

"Why, yes," I reply, surprised.

"Well, I thought so, you are so young," he mused. "My wife died a year ago, and now I'm looking for a new wife. The problem is that I worry that when I find her, I'll compare her to my wife of 30 years, and she won't be the same."

"She won't be," I reply. "But for your second 30-year-marriage, you might want some changes anyway."

He grins. "Why, of course! I never thought of that. I'll keep looking." He bows slightly, turns quickly, and walks on, appearing as if he will do a Fred Astaire jump and click his heels in mid-air.

He'll find someone by nightfall, I'm convinced. On a spring day like this, why not?

April 14, 1980

Mini-Vacation

Arizona sun shines through the palms
The day snuggles in like a babe in arms
The one-eyed morning expands
I'm away
Nothing presses this miniscule day
No Saturday cartoons bombard my dreams
Do the children have bread, cereal, cream?
No puppy at 6 a.m. can bark
Will the people complain across the park?
My space is empty
   Palettes and tables bare
   Pings of homebound concern
   dissipate quickly to the air.
At home I shun such vacuums
   A day dawning unstructured clear
   Time too short to waste a minute!
   What to do to add my bit!
   Nothingness?? A creeping fear—
   Action above all, don't slow down—
   Keep yourself in a twit.
Homebound days do not allow
   The vacuum to surround
   Which I feel now.
The hole and the whole wrap me
   in cotton gossamer wings

I take you total nothingness
And my heart sings.
I don't have to jog—
     but I may.
I don't have to write—
     but I can.
I don't have to read—
     but I probably will.
This minute I just luxuriate in
     the quiet; the still.
Nature abhors a vacuum
     Not me.
Today I love nothingness
     Passionately.

March 1, 1982

VIII: Friendships and Relationships

For those who have found "rugged individualism" a much touted myth—

No man [or woman] is an island entire of itself.
John Donne

Building Friendships

"Do you want to be friends?"

When one was little, it was easy to ask that question of another 4-year-old child. The process, however, becomes more complicated as one grows older. One grows afraid of appearing foolish, like a blundering would-be lover, afraid of rejection. Or, conversely, one may fear acceptance, cautiously enumerating in advance the entanglements a new relationship could involve. "By definition friendship is inconvenient," writes columnist Melvin Maddox.

Yet, it's scary how easily, because of circumstances—distance, inconvenience, divorce—friends slip out of our lives.

"Blood is thicker than water," say the sages, reminding us that family is our first and last real friend. Yes, but blood is also stickier, and it is sometimes only the "watering" from nonrelated friends that can allow unexpressed parts of us to flower.

Friendships once were formed early in life and sustained by mutual daily activities or by letters. When one reads the letters between Susan and Augusta in Wallace Stegner's *Angle of Repose* or those of Bess to her beloved friend Totsie in Elizabeth Forsythe Hailey's *Woman of Independent*

Means, one cannot help but experience a thread of ink, strong as steel, that bound friends over time, over issues, and over miles.

Today that thread is more likely to be a phone cord. No matter. The psychic connection is the same. "I was just thinking about that!" is my almost inevitable response when one close friend spontaneously calls long distance to converse.

The feminist movement's revalidation of the intense personal friendship between women has restored to many of us a part of our selves we have neglected. Yet, deep friendships also create certain ambivalences which were not present in the '50s and '60s, back when it was simply "understood" by women friends that male-female relationships came first.

One may become angry at and resentful of unexpected and unaccepted friendship roles. Often, as in marriage, the parameters of the friendship relationship need to be defined and redefined by the people involved. One woman, slowly, painfully, explained to her friend that she could not provide all the help she would like to for her friend's children, terrible as she felt about the divorce; she could not become the "second parent." To the woman's relief, her friend heard her and understood.

Another woman, exhausted by her friend's acquaintances, said, "I want to see you any time you come to town, but I really can't meet with everyone close to you that you want me to get to know, okay?"

"Okay." Again, relief on both sides.

Relief, of course, is not guaranteed. Sometimes a friend will cling to a certain expectation or definition of loyalty which is not acceptable to the other partner. When the terms of a friendship are renegotiated, the bonds can either grow and strengthen or stretch and snap.

"Do you want to be friends?" Whatever adult jargon we say it in, are close friendships still worth the time, the emotion, the redefinition and the fear of loss involved? Yes.

Writing this immediately after lingering an extra hour

over lunch with a close friend, I am warmed by the fact that that extra hour—already playing havoc with my tightly scheduled day—will immeasurably enrich my life.

"Neither love nor friendship are fit subjects for time and motion studies," Melvin Maddox wrote. "If we really want efficiency, we'll just have to opt for no waste, no manipulation, loneliness and get it over with."

August 24, 1981

Friendships with Other Women Have Evolved Slowly and Gracefully

She was blonde, slender, clear-skinned, and ethereal— beautiful in the eyes of her dorm mates as well as all the men on campus. Of the latter, she could have dated any of them at any time. Yet, she willingly would turn down or even break a date if a roommate or a girlfriend needed her. The rest of us loved her, but couldn't understand her.

Some of us, who had an unspoken but tacit agreement that a date—any date—would take precedence over strictly female affairs, were even suspicious of her. What was she trying to prove? Was she running for dorm president? It was then 1955.

In retrospect, I view her as being about 20 years ahead of her time. She placed a value on female friendship that many of us haven't been able to do until our 40s.

A recent *U.S. News and World Report* article on stress and chronic fatigue expresses a popularly held view: "In our culture women seem to be more willing to talk about what hurts than men." I wonder. It may be true currently, but for me, it was a long time coming.

I think about all of this now because 1979 is becoming a strange and wonderful year of reunions with old friends: a three-hour lunch with a grammar-school pal who just moved to Colorado; the deepening and expanding correspondence with a former stewardess roommate; an intense meeting with a woman from my high school which resulted from the death of a mutual friend. And we are reuniting on such a vastly different level! Husbands, children, and their achievements are the usual openers; but the sharing of our own accomplishments, dreams, frustrations, and failures are quick to follow. The defensiveness and competition of the old days is dwindling or totally absent.

What did we talk of in the old days? It's hard to recall. Times with roommates were warm, fun, spontaneous, and sometimes hilarious. Friendships evolved from shared experiences, but shared feelings were as absent as they purportedly were with males of the same generation. If one was happy, one was part of the group; if one cried, one went to one's room as a child often is instructed to do.

To be successful and "cool" were the mottos of the day. We, as well as our male counterparts, were preoccupied with getting, getting dates, getting good grades, getting tan, getting thin, getting married, or getting into graduate school. Totally upwardly mobile, we peeked warily over the edges of our defenses, ready always with a practiced grin to hide any pain.

Later, even casual friendships seemed to dwindle. So preoccupied with reproducing, helping husbands forge ahead, moving and balancing work life and family, we seemed to have no choice but to keep our own counsel.

Liv Ullmann, in her published personal journal *Changing*, describes a long corridor in the house in which she and Ingmar Bergman lived after their infant daughter was born. At one end of the house was "he who sat in his study and wanted to own me alone! At the other end was she who could barely walk, and who cried for me. . . . I rushed from one to the other with a bad conscience never able completely to give what I yearned to receive."

I see myself and my friends in those years rushing up and down our own private corridors, pushing away our own private conflicts, our desperately needed friendships reduced to recipe sharing.

But the high point in my series of recent reunions was a ski vacation on which I met an old friend from out of state with whom I had chatted euphorically by long distance for many years. Going up on the chairlift, she confided in me: "Things weren't really all that great when the kids were little," she said. "In fact, I was in therapy for two years."

"You, too!" I exploded. "What years?"

We laughed hysterically; we then came close to tears when we discovered we had been depressed at exactly the same time. "Look how much time and money we could have saved, if we had only shared these things with each other!" my friend exclaimed. We can talk now, really talk; but we couldn't then and we're still not sure why.

"Maybe 'getting' as opposed to giving and receiving is a necessary mind-set of the young," said a member of my women's group when we were discussing the issue of emotional sharing. "Maybe now with the counterculture of the '60s, the women's movement and the increased sharing of parental roles, young people are becoming more open. But I still think we're more likely to mellow when we're past 40," she continued. "And I'm glad I'm past!"

So am I.

June 18, 1979

Empathy May Be the Essence of Support

"I want more support from my husband," complained a young married friend of mine. "But he thinks of support only in terms of money and doesn't know what I'm talking about."

Support, support systems, emotional support. The word "support" has become overused to the point that it can mean anything, or nothing. "Support systems" might be defined as any set of formal or informal community networks that reduce the hassle of everyday life and may or may not include emotional succor or financial exchange. For example, a friendly neighbor with kids the age of one's own, a live-in babysitter, a grocery store within walking distance, a bus stop near one's corner, a boss who lets you set your own hours, a competent secretary, a reliable once-a-week housekeeper.

"Emotional support" is a phrase even more elusive. "Caring" is too general, although caring is involved. Caring people give advice, but advice is not always supportive. Listening may be more in order.

Is emotional support unconditional love and acceptance? Perhaps, but support is also constructive criticism. "My stepson comes to me when he wants support," says a friend of mine. "He knows I'll tell him the truth, whereas his father is afraid of hurting his feelings."

True support is not overly indulgent or eternally sympathetic. It does not say, "I hear where you are hurting and failing, and how awful!" Nor does it say, "I hear where you are hurting and failing and you shouldn't." Instead it says "I hear where you are hurting and failing, and you will rise from that place and move on."

And perhaps the essence of support is letting a troubled person know that you feel the same way, or if you don't, letting him or her know of someone else who does.

Recently, two women I have come to know through the women's movement told me of the first time they had read Bretty Freidan's book, *The Feminine Mystique*. Josie Heath, formerly regional head of Action, recalled, "I was an army wife stationed in Germany doing lots of reading while taking care of my first baby. I thought Betty really had something there; but there was no one I could talk to to see if other women felt this way, or if it was just she and me!"

Mary Hoagland, attorney at law, recalled with irony: "I was having my fourth child and very involved with my community. I really identified with what Friedan said, but when I mentioned it to a friend, she said, 'You couldn't possibly agree with her! How can you be listening to someone like that!' Her one comment was such a putdown it scared me out of getting involved in the women's movement for another several years."

These two episodes give rise to a vision of hundreds of baby-tending, 1964-era homemakers immediately identifying with Friedan, yet unable or afraid to discuss this new identity. "In sociology [it's] called pluralistic ignorance when many people are experiencing the same thing but nobody knows it," says Frank Furstenberg, University of Pennsylvania sociologist. And "pluralistic ignorance" runs rampant when we bite our tongues because we perceive that what we as individuals are experiencing may run counter to the accepted modes of the dominant culture; though each of us in her "ignorance" may rapidly be becoming the dominant culture.

Who can give support? Not only women to each other, and women to men. But men to women, and more increasingly, according to a *New York Times* article by Enid Nemy, men to men. One man, a successful international lawyer interviewed by Ms. Nemy, observed that "during the last few months almost all of my lunch companions have, at some point, veered away from business, and started discussing their own lives." And from a male sales executive in the same article, "Maybe the conversation doesn't mean anything in itself, but it's the idea that you feel free to have the conversation that's important. That 'stiff upper lip' is vastly overrated."

Men, in recent years, probably have been much more emotionally supportive within their families and to each other than they have been given credit for. What (up until now) has prevented them from admitting such and being given the credit?

Pluralistic ignorance, I suspect.

August 18, 1980

What Old Friends Are All About

Last spring we had dinner with another couple, two of our closest friends. It was in one of those restaurants with cubbyholes, the kind that insures privacy—the adventure of dining out with the intimacy of staying home.

After we had ordered wine, I spontaneously related a small personal success experience I had had just that day. Sitting in a warm glow, as the conversation then bounced from the earthshaking to the trivial and back—as it does with friends who are effortlessly comfortable with one another—I mused on just what was so special about this friendship.

Not so different really from those other special friendships made over many years. Enough time, shared experiences, similar philosophies, and even that circumstantial, though sometimes crucial, ingredient of convenience: children who are friends, too.

Old friends are valuable in the way new friends have yet to become. They are irreplaceable in the sense that Antoine de St. Exupery captures so eloquently: "Old friends cannot be created out of hand. Nothing can match the treasure of common memories, of trials endured together, of quarrels and reconciliations and generous emotions. It is idle, having planted an acorn in the morning, to expect that afternoon to sit in the shade of the oak."

Yet, with this "old" friendship there exists an added dimension. When the four of us get together more is created than merely exchanged. We are catalysts for each other, and in each other's presence share not only what we know, but things we didn't know we knew until we came together.

Without this particular friendship I might never have told that little story which gave me so many "strokes" in the telling. It would have been tasteless in a large group, boring to children at a family dinner, and hardly a burning enough issue to interrupt other strictly spousal conversation with, "By the way . . ."

Perhaps a further dynamic of such a friendship is the fresh insight the foursome relationship provides to each individual spouse about the other, insight which stimulates a new "couples-closeness" which might have been missed even in a romantic evening alone.

Really close friends have a way of bringing up a touchy subject one may have avoided with one's spouse. All of a sudden, with a silent sigh of relief, there it is—right on the table—defined and ultimately approachable. When my husband and I left the restaurant that night, we embraced our friends goodbye, then walked away closer and more connected than when we walked in.

Near the end of the movie *The Four Seasons*, the character played by Carol Burnett alludes to the fear that without friends we'd just "end up old, the two of us, against the world." Perhaps even worse; without friends, we couples might end up "the one and the other of us," against the world. Devoted, yet separate and lonely.

October 12, 1981

Interlude of Warmth and Reflection

The interlude between Christmas and New Year's Day is a quiet time. A time for reflecting on the past, planning for the future, and reading our Christmas messages. As I read, I am flooded with a feeling of warmth and a sense of gratitude for old friendships.

Our best friends, Phil and Susan, just had their first grandchild. Their son, whom we remember cooing loudly while his father stretched him to a standing position on his knees at the age of three months, is all grown up. Now he has his own son.

The 20-some years we've known Phil and Susan parade by like flashbacks in a silent movie.

1962: They lived in Washington, D.C. We, not yet married, lived in Denver. They visited us for a trip in the mountains and to hear Joan Baez at Red Rocks. Susan and I fried chicken in Dick's apartment. Phil and Dick forgot to put it in the car. We ate popcorn at the concert.

1963: They had their first child. We married and visited them in Washington on our way to South America. We slept, roasting in our down sleeping bags, in their backyard

in July. They had a party. The only woman from Phil and
Dick's law school class came. Imagine! A woman attorney!

Phil's brother died of a heart attack at 41. We visited their
family. We were awkward and ill at ease. It was our first
experience with death at middle age.

1967: Our first child arrived. Phil and Susan visited us in
Denver. It was January. It snowed. Phil and Susan ran
outside in wonder. It doesn't snow in San Jose, California,
where they now lived. Susan told me our son needed formula to supplement breast feedings, if I wanted to get him to
sleep through the night. She was right.

1970-1973: Now we had two children and they had three.
We rendezvoused at their beach house in Santa Cruz. It was
crowded and the kids woke us up early. The steps from the
beach to the beachhouse stretched upward like Jacob's ladder. Our daughter had to be carried, cautiously, tediously,
each step. Our son played in the cold Pacific Ocean like it
was a warm bath. I wore an orange bikini. Our daughter got
sunburned. We went for ice cream one night after dinner.
Five children's faces smeared with chocolate, peach, pep-
permint, and pistachio. We laughed so hard, their youngest
boy cried. I wish we had a picture.

1974: Our visits became less frequent, and long phone
calls filled the gap. Phil ran for the school board. Dick ran
for governor. Their whole family came out to help us in the
primary.

1975-1982: Their first son had his Bar Mitzvah and took
up football. Their daughter had her Bas Mitzvah and took up
photography, then baseball. Our daughter took up ice skating. Our son took up scuba diving. I took up journalism.
Their second son had his Bar Mitzvah. Their first son was
married. Phil finished his school board term. Dick ran for a
third term as governor. Susan ran for City Council.

And now, their first son is balancing his first son on his
knees, as his father had balanced him. And the 20 years feel
like one.

When I was a child people always told me that the years go

faster the older you get. I'm now 45. What will the next 20 years seem like—a month?

Time passes. And if one is lucky, friendships deepen. Time flies. And until someone is born or dies, we forget.

December 27, 1982

Woman's Role as Communicator

The governors' wives were really turned on to the subject! Their lively dialogue on family communication burst forth honest, frustrated, creative, grappling, and sometimes angry.

This interchange, unburdened by the presence of press and security guards, was real. This was earnest. This was special. The recent communications seminar in Washington, D.C., was the best program to come out of the National Governors' Conference spouses' organization in eight years. Yet, something seemed slightly off, out of whack, not quite right. Something was being taken for granted that shouldn't have been, but what was it?

That night in the Hyatt Regency Hotel my eyes fell on Ellen Goodman's column in the *Washington Post*. Reading the column, I suddenly realized what "it" was. Goodman wrote of the communications role of a close female friend: "The people in her home communicate with each other through her. She delivers peace messages from one child to another. Softens ultimatums from father to son; explains the daughter to father. Under her constant monitoring, the communication lines are kept open; one person stays plugged into the next."

Goodman continued, "But sometimes I wonder whether she has kept all of these people together or whether she has kept them apart. Does she make it easier for them to understand each other or does she actually stand between them, holding all the wires in her hand?"

And, finally, "I know it is a skill to be able to understand and analyze one person's motives and psyche to another. It requires time, attention, emotional dexterity to run these switchboards. Yet, it can also overload the operator and cripple the people from talking across their own private lines."

Communication—a woman's job. Switchboard operating— a woman's trap. There we all were at that meeting taking responsibility. Again, we had tacitly accepted the premise that it was as much our role to grapple with new communication techniques as it was for our husbands to struggle with the "New Federalism."

Like Goodman, I agree that communication is a skill, and that sometimes we women need to explain a father's discipline to a son, so that he can receive it in a softer way. Sometimes we need to keep a family reunion peaceful by reminding each member in private what another may be expecting of them. Sometimes it is absolutely necessary to explain to a father an adolescent girl's behavior, drawing on our own experience as a girl years before.

But, also like Goodman, I think sometimes maybe we need to let go. We need to let our loved ones explain themselves, or not explain themselves, to other loved ones in their own ways. We need to let family members confront each other in awkward and sometimes angry modes that can shatter the peace. Occasionally we need to drop the connecting wires that emanate from our head, our heart, and our gut, and see what new family communication patterns will emerge without us.

Knowing when to connect the wires and when to drop them is one of the new dilemmas of choice we women have won for ourselves. If we no longer take it as a given that we always will assume the prescribed role of traditional "peacemaker," we have to decide each situation on its own merits. And that's much harder. Sometimes we make the wrong choice. Sometimes the results are complicated.

Once, a dozen years ago, at a large family gathering, I had an inner sense that I was the only one who could smooth the antagonistic ripples lurking under the waves of forced joviality. But I was tired, and I refused. I dropped the wires and went to bed. The short-term effect of my neglect was nearly disastrous, and I felt guilty for weeks. But over time, springing from that incident, new communication patterns formed; healthier family relationships slowly and tentatively emerged, all of which are more or less entrenched today.

It's scary and risky for women, early trained to be peacemakers, to pull back from the switchboard, to drop the connecting wires that might energize a potential peace. You never know what the results of an action will be until you try. Or perhaps you never know until you stop trying. And sometimes you don't know if you made the right decision till years later.

April 5, 1982

Are Caring and Concern Turned On and Off When It Seems Convenient?

"Is your headache gone?" he asked suddenly. His eyes flashed with concern as he looked away, embarrassed both by the intensity of his caring and by the fact that he had forgotten for so long. The woman smiled, any remaining irritation almost washed away by his solicitousness. She had told her husband of the pounding in her head at the beginning of the climb down the sun-baked slope—a trail lost in crumbling, red rocks which soaked in the heat and radiated it back. But he hadn't heard, she thought. He was, as so often, lost in some distant thoughts.

Two hours she struggled down, backpack awkwardly swaying, unbalancing each tentative step from rock to rock, the sweat pouring from under her hat and the top of her lip. He had not asked how she was doing in those two hours. Only occasionally had he looked back. Yet now, as they crunched through the needle-strewn paths and level trails of the pine forest, now, as the going grew so easy, the throbbing in her head had given way to the sound of crickets, birds, and an occasional lonely coyote. Now, his voice broke through nature's silence with his sudden concern.

Husbands are concerned when they happen to think of it; wives are concerned when their husbands need them, she parroted to herself, the old irritation again rising in her throat. But there was a knee-jerk flavor to her reaction, a conditioned response without its full power, and along with it a nagging uneasiness, a jarring remembrance of something close, something personal, that made her judgment of him ring unfair.

"Are you sure you are feeling all right?" Her own voice came back to her from the previous week. The woman was a professional person, and she had been fortunate enough to find a superbly talented secretary-research assistant.

"What every wife needs is a really good wife!" The woman and her assistant had joked about that saying. They were friends; yet somehow the structure of their boss/assistant working relationship had slowly, almost imperceptibly, become similar to that of husband/wife. She would initiate; her assistant would follow. She would "care," expressing it when caring fit her schedule, her assistant would "care" when her boss needed her to. She would talk about her problems when she felt like it; her assistant talked of her problems when the timing was right—only if she were sure her boss was in the right mood.

Last week they had been researching a project that entailed sitting on the floor, sorting, and collating items in stacks. Her assistant had told her previously that certain backache troubles made it difficult for her to sit in one place too long. But that day, they had sat cross-legged for two hours, the woman totally lost in the content of the project, her curiosity of what the ultimate findings would show consuming every nerve. It was only when they were done that she had remembered.

"Your back! Are you sure you are feeling all right?" she asked her assistant, with the same intensity, that same embarrassment, that same expression which on her husband's face had prompted her feeling of *déjà vu*.

Back in the woods, the couple neared a sun-streaked clearing, the camp spot they sought. The woman's husband turned around to find her shaking her head and silently laughing to herself.

"What are you grinning so secretly about?" he asked as he set down his pack and offered to help her with hers.

"I'm grinning," she said, "because I've found I'm so much like you."

July 27, 1981

IX: Emotions—Love, Frustration, Anger, Grief

For those who burst with laughter, tears, or trauma—but sometimes dare not show it—

For only that which is deeply felt can change us.

Marilyn Ferguson

How Do I Love Thee? Let Me Count the Ways

For the three days my former college dorm-mate stayed with us, we talked about her marriage—its high, its lows, its ultimate failure. We talked about communication and lack of it; intimacy and its difficulty. We blamed his "macho," her assertiveness, and the magical expectations of coming to age in the '50s.

It was not till the third day that she mentioned it; and she did so almost offhandedly. Emotionally spent with analysis of the relationship, exhausted by uncovering each regret, she sighed with resignation. "I guess," she said, "I was never really in love with him."

Love. Romantic love. Marital love. Exalted in great classics such as *Romeo and Juliet*, made trivial by the plethora of romance magazines; yet, in the week before Valentine's Day as I checked through my files on Feminism, Family, Psychology, and Sex Roles, I found little on love.

There were lots of articles regarding the marital relationships of working wives, "helpful" husbands, female breadwinners, and male homemakers. But love? Nothing. Perhaps, heaven forbid, I have "selected out" the subject. Perhaps I need a new filing system. Or possibly I find little, because little is written.

Only Phyllis Volkens' wonderfully personal, "I am Blessed and Truly Loved," (*Denver Post*, August 22, 1980) stands out as pertinent: "Love, I didn't know mortals could love like this, so completely unconditional, no games or strings. [My husband] sees all my faults, but he loves me as though I had none."

Love is difficult to talk about, even between couples who share it. It takes Tevye and Golde 25 years of marriage in *Fiddler on the Roof.* "Do you love me?" Tevye persists. "After 25 years, I suppose I do," is Golde's final admission. For them, as for many of us, it's easier to talk about the milk horse, the daughters, the Sabbath, and the laundry.

Today, everything from perversion to death is grist for the conversational mill, yet the word love still can bring a blush, especially to those of us approaching or leaving middle age. If in love with our spouses, we fear appearing too sentimental. If not in love with our spouses, we fear the depression that could come with such admission, or a vague sense of shame at others finding out.

"Love is not enough," wrote child psychologist Bruno Bettelheim. He was writing of parents and children. But his phrase applies to marriage, too. Love, in itself, may not be enough to overcome widely divergent cultural backgrounds, grossly unequal workloads, the stultification of one's partner's personal growth, or devastating economic deprivation. But is it possible we read about, write about, weigh, and become obsessed with the potentially divisive down sides of a relationship because we are afraid to put on the scale that crucial ingredient of whether or not we are really in love?

Perhaps we don't talk about it because only poets don't tremble when they try to put such delicately savored feelings to words:

That certain premonition telling us that *her* footstep is approaching through a noisy crowd.

That happy exhilaration that catches us unaware and rails against our logic as *his* wheels crunch up the driveway in the snow—even though we thought we were furious with him and may still be.

That lightness and dizziness which suddenly, spontaneously reanoints a couple with delight, after days or even weeks of bumping about and mucking through the maze of household trivia.

Love may not be able to overcome our "big" marital problems. But without its force—which suddenly can render us sexy, sensitive, or quixotically silly—will we even be motivated to work out the little ones? Love very well may not be enough. But is marriage "enough" without it?

March 2, 1981

Why Apologize Over a Few Tears?

"I spent the first two days crying in the third-floor closet," said the wife of a newly elected governor as she told of her tension-filled move into their state's governor's mansion.

"But *we* wouldn't do that, would we?" said my aunt pointedly, when just before our own family made its big move, I told her my new friend's story.

Crying: a dilemma—whether or not to. It's healthy; it's weak. It's OK for "big" things. It's not OK in public. It's OK for females. Big boys don't cry.

Edmund Muskie's angry public tears over criticism directed at his wife might have cost him the 1972 Democratic nomination for president. Adlai Stevenson's classic remark, "I feel like the boy who stubbed his toe. I'm too big to cry, but it hurts too much to laugh," might best exemplify the emotional paradox of all Americans over age 10. One suspects Adlai Stevenson did cry, at least in private, when, in 1956, he lost the presidency for the second time.

We tend to think of crying as a purely emotional release. Yet biochemist William H. Frey has found that "shedding tears relieves the body of toxic chemicals produced by emotional stress." So crying might be a health tonic for the body as well as for the spirit. "Even the common cold may be

brought on by the failure to cry," reports *Ms.* magazine.
And Frey suggests that "the social prohibition against men
crying may contribute to their high incidence of stress-
related disorders."

When we recall the religious persecution and the physical
hardships suffered by the early Puritans who settled
America, we can understand their adherence to the "stiff
upper lip," the need to be finely honed and non-emotional at
all times. And we have inherited much of their stoicism. We
bury our dead and keep on working, the couple in the famed
painting *American Gothic* by Grant Wood seems to say.
One can actually feel them slipping out of the frame to a
back-breaking, 12-hour day of uncomplaining toil, never a
tear to be shed.

But our life expectancies now range between 70 and 80
years, rather than between 50 and 60 years as they did in
Grant Wood's time—20 years longer for those toxic chemicals to build up. Is it possible that if we won't let ourselves
cry, we are living our lives longer but enjoying them less?

Other experts tell us crying isn't always healthy. In the
early 1970s, I participated in an assertiveness training workshop for women. Our leader made us practice "dry-eyed
anger." Each of us was to argue with a partner over an
emotional issue; in "steely-eyed verbal conciseness" we
were to "fight" with our opponent without succumbing to
tears.

"Crying," said our leader, "can not only cause you to lose,
but can decrease the strength of your body and your self-
image. Giving in to tears merely reinforces a woman's feeling of helplessness in a male dominant society."

And the stereotyped female crying for calculated ends is
the unhealthiest crying of all. Or is it? I know another
political wife, generally cheerful and nonmanipulative, who
on one occasion burst into tears over an issue position her
husband was about to announce. "It allowed him to change
his mind and to save face," she said to me coolly. "He knew
it was wrong, I knew it was wrong. He couldn't admit to me

it was wrong. But he could turn on his heel and do an instant change of direction 'in order to make me happy.' "

What message do we give our children about crying? A mixed one, I imagine. My mother-in-law once told my irritable, cranky, sniffling, sobbing 6-year-old to save his tears for the important things in life, the times he would really need them. It worked, he stopped immediately, appreciating her simple logic.

Save your tears for the important times, as if tears are limited or exhaustible like our present supplies of gasoline. A sound and practical philosophy. But who decides what is "important"? Death and desertion are usually "permissible" times for crying even in the most stoic segments of our society. Yet, a friend of mine who just returned from a favorite uncle's funeral said that her aunt, who broke down briefly at her husband's interment, apologized for her weakness and admonished the other relatives to be stronger. "It was as if the past reputation and future glory of New England depended upon her family's stoicism," said my friend.

Crying children irritate us the most when we feel caught by the same vulnerabilities they feel but are ashamed to admit it. Once my daughter and I were caught in a wet, miserable, face-stinging snowstorm while skiing. We were in no physical danger; we knew the way down, so there was no need for heroics or courage in conquering the elements. But I was determined to hold a stiff (as well as cold) upper lip.

As my daughter sobbed her way down the mountain, I grew increasingly angry with her. It was not her character I feared for, but my own parental loss of pride. My anger was simply envy transformed; I was jealous of her 7-year-old freedom to "let go."

August 4, 1980

There Are No Easy Rules for Coping with Anger

In the late 1960s when I worked as a psychiatric social worker at the University of Colorado Health Sciences Center, the subject of anger dominated most staff meetings and at least half of my client therapy sessions. What was the client angry about? How did she/he express it? Repress it? Transfer it? Own up to it? Get rid of it?

(*Just a minute . . . my 15-year-old is yelling at me.*)

It generally was assumed that one would not be in therapy if one was not angry. It also was assumed that expressing it was better than repressing it, at least in the therapeutic hour.

What the person, client or therapist, did with angry feelings outside the therapeutic hour was more complicated. As I read a *Psychology Today* excerpt of Carol Tavris' new book *Anger: The Misunderstood Emotion*, I perceive that the misunderstood emotion has not become any less complicated over the past decade.

(*He's still yelling so loudly I can't understand what he wants!*)

Tavris pokes holes in some highly touted pop psychology cliches about anger:

Cliche Number One: Direct hostile expression of anger leads to better mental health and reduced stress. Not always, says Tavris. In fact, there is direct evidence to the contrary. Research done by a social psychologist reveals that when college-age males retaliate against a fellow student or another "peer" with direct anger, stress is reduced, but not when they retaliate against a teacher or another symbol of authority.

(*Have I become a "peer"? . . . I must reassert my authority.*)

A sociologist who studies family violence finds that couples who yell at each other feel more angry afterward, not less. The "Type A" personality who "swears impatiently at delays, and flares into aggression or hostility at the slightest chance" is more susceptible to heart disease than his more controlled or reflective counterpart. A child who is allowed unfettered angry and aggressive behavior becomes more anxious or angry, not less.

(*A good parent would stop this ridiculous outburst!*)

Cliche Number 2: Talking out one's anger with friends or a therapist will help dissipate the feeling. Only sometimes. "The belief that talking it out is cathartic assumes that there is a single emotion to be released," writes Tavris. Yet anger is usually mixed with hurt, jealousy, fear, sadness, and guilt.

(*What's really behind all this noise?*)

We all have experienced stress reduction by talking over these complex feelings with friends or with people in the helping professions. But if we express only the anger, and get support for only the anger, we aren't ventilating the anger, we are rehearsing it. One could expect to leave such an encounter more furious than one entered it.

(*Sure sounds like he's rehearsing it! What for?*)

Cliche Number Three: Handling anger is a pure and simple task devoid of cultural or class input. Hardly ever. "The connection between anger (expressed or suppressed) and high blood pressure depends on your age, race, sex, social class and primarily on the reason you feel angry." Women are more likely to reduce stress by the conversion of anger to friendly feelings, working out a problem by soothing or negotiation.

(*I don't feel like negotiating—not now.*)

A majority of working class men in Detroit reported that if treated unfairly on the job, they would protest to the boss directly or report him to someone higher up. Yet, these assertive men were more likely to develop high blood pressure than their peers who would shrug off injustice. Especially vulnerable to stress were the assertive young black men living in ghetto neighborhoods with high unemployment.

(*At last. He's calming down. . . . I hear the problem. Maybe I can help. . . .*)

The key to release of tension and better health, says Tavris, is dependent not so much on if you express your anger directly, but what you do to confront the irritating situation. "Does whatever you do with your anger help restore control over your life?"

(*He's calling his antagonist—an adult—on the phone. I shut my eyes and pray.*)

Just because ventilating is not as healthy as once thought, Tavris does not recommend endless suppression. "Silent sulking is a lousy and deadly weapon." The crimes of violence committed after which relatives and neighbors say of the accused, "But he was such a nice quiet boy," testifies to this. Pretending everything is fine is not going to reduce feelings of anger.

(*He's facing the problem—nicely, calmly, maturely. Where did the anger go?*)

"The purpose of anger is to make a grievance known—to change some injustice in your environment." If we are in a job, a relationship, or a social stratum that provokes us and we cannot or will not change it, ameliorate it, or leave it, we are most susceptible to physical symptoms of stress. "If the grievance is not confronted, it will not matter whether the anger is kept in, let out or wrapped in red ribbons and dropped in the Erie Canal," Tavris warns.

(*Could he have been as calm confronting his antagonist if he had not first "dropped" his anger on me?*)

Anger. There's much about it we still don't understand.

February 21, 1983

Accentuate the Positive—But Face the Negative, Too!

A friend of mine is into "positive" astrology. Trained in the ways of the sun, moon, and stars, she says, "I only translate to people the positive signs I see. The negatives will take care of themselves."

An artist I am acquainted with tells me that the Indians he has grown to know through his work read bones and skulls in only a positive way. No "bad luck" signs are seen or interpreted.

In the ever-expanding optimism of American culture, the "power of positive thinking" has become almost cliche. Ignore and repress the negative and it will just go away. But does it?

I tried these methods recently when recovering from breast cancer surgery. I dared not think of the remaining cancer cells that might still be in my body. To do so would give them power to grow, I reasoned. I dared not read any negative statistics. Denial worked for a while. Then a well-meaning person sent me a depressing article about cancer. I read it without reading it, related to it without absorbing it, held it at arm's distance but couldn't quite let go.

The article sat on the peripheral rim of my mind, but I would not encapture it. My fears screamed, "Go away! Go away!" But it didn't. My faith screamed, "Concentrate on the positive!" But I couldn't.

Suddenly I was no longer in a positive place but in limbo. All my energies were tied up in not dealing with that article. Two sleepless nights ensued. During one I tried to rid my fears by reading novels; the other I tried writing on subjects unrelated to my illness. But work, the great panacea for depression, failed. Finally, I knew I must draw close those sheets of paper with sad stories and negative statistics. So I did, at 2 a.m., shivering under a night light. I cried.

I went to the kitchen, huddled on a stool, and cried some more. Panic-stricken, I entered the tunnel of my own death—I saw my weeping children, heard eulogies at my funeral—and came out the other end. As I wrapped my flowered flannel hospital robe around me tightly, the shivering and the crying suddenly stopped. I'd seen the worst. I'd encountered my possible demise. I'd been as far down as I could go. Now there was only one way: up.

I reached for milk and cookies. I filled the tub and took a long, luxurious bath in the glow of the nightlights and the sound of classical music. I was no longer depressed, not even "positive," but just plain happy. Happy I was as well as I was. Thankful for my family and my friends. Sobered only by the realization that others in my situation had neither medical care nor love. Concerned, finally, about someone besides myself.

A friend sent me the following quote shortly after I left the hospital: "When fear knocks at the door, faith answers." Yes, but for me, faith only answers when I first let fear over the doorstep and wrestle with it. Others may be able to slam the door on fear when facing trauma, but for me, facing death was the only way to return to life.

December 14, 1981

A Hard Year, with Many Blessings

Columnist Ellen Goodman writes succinctly of the oft-conflicting burdens and challenges greeting the middle-aged person. "Middle-age has both aging parents and adolescent children. Middle-age has bosses to please and deadlines to meet and bills to pay. Middle-age sometimes feel useful, strong, sturdy, and sometimes feels overwhelmed."

Yet, how these responsibilities, especially the human ones, can in an instant become a support system when middle-age turns ill, when suddenly the "middle-ager" turns into patient. As the mid-point of my 45th year and Thanksgiving approach in rapid succession I find myself, not burdened by middle-age, but instead counting its numerous blessings.

What a blessing to have a 10-year-old daughter who cuts beneath the fear and brings out the family's sense of humor by linking the immediate and the trivial with the immortal. When I entered the hospital in late August, she exclaimed: "You're going to the hospital. (Gasp.) But who'll take me on my back-to-school shopping trip?" And, "You're going to the hospital. (Gasp.) Mom, are you going to die?"

Returning from the hospital, what a blessing to have a

teenage son who, with a friend, spent a glorious Indian Summer Saturday not riding bikes or passing Frisbees but baking poppyseed bread in a stuffy kitchen. "We want to do something for you, Mom," he said.

What a blessing to have a husband who spent the night calling around the country making sure I was getting the best medical care. Who brought me not his own political hassles in the morning, but a self-penned poem to my recovery.

What a blessing to have in-laws who arrived after an exhausting auto trip and immediately smoothed the household routine, giving me solitude and privacy.

What a blessing to have a mother who welcomed me home to the town in which I grew up, and who, having borne my illness far harder than I, brought me tea in bed while I wrote poetry; who cared for me till we both felt better.

What a blessing to have a sister who postponed 10 days of pressing academic work to be the telephone communicator keeping countless relatives and friends reassured and advised of my condition.

What a blessing to have friends—all old enough to have had griefs of their own—who knew what I was going through.

What a blessing to have bosses and colleagues willing to give me time, taking the pressure off, easing the deadline, even though I didn't need it.

What a blessing to be middle-aged, when the "charges" you care for, who often appear to take you for granted, suddenly turn solicitous and tender, eyes shining with love.

November 23, 1981

Dealing with Death

Late last winter a 53-year-old woman named Jeanne Boone who had lost her 28-year-old daughter, Lari, to a recurring and debilitating illness wrote me the following: "You have a forum with which you can reach others. Do you suppose you could address this subject of losing a loved one to death in a column? Could you ask others how they have dealt or how they are dealing? Perhaps you know on a personal basis. . . ."

Although I answered the letter, I repressed the request. I had just written one column dealing with cancer and another on the deaths of five young people, killed by drunk drivers. I did not want my weekly column to become a repository only for the catastrophic.

Then last summer, the subject came back to me, first through a discussion I had with 20 Gold Star Mothers, and second through a booklet sent to me by a South High School teacher whose 17-year-old student, Paul Garver, had died of cancer. The booklet, written predominantly by Susan Garver, Paul's mother, made me realize how useful such a column might be.

Susan Garver began her long ordeal of grief with a night alone in the mountains: "Yea, I did it! I spent the night in the wilderness alone. I wanted to come to a place with strong memories of Paul and his courage, so I drove to the Indian Peaks wilderness area where Paul, at the age of 8, had led me up Mount Audubon in spite of my acrophobia. . . .

"Last night I had been so fearful at one moment I couldn't see a thing! A pine marten had run through my camp. . . . My fear of a wild animal tearing me apart unwitnessed was overwhelming until I thought of Paul's courage facing death. . . . He wished as natural a death as possible, at home, in his own bed, with his parents, sister, and friends by his side and no props. . . . How could I be fearful when the stars emerged.

"The Milky Way was directly overhead with its myriad of stars to ponder. Paul was up there somewhere! I know that Paul would not want me to grieve too much over his young death, but rather to continue loving and caring for people as a wife, mother, teacher, friend."

John Garver, Paul's father, used poetry to express his pain:

My garden flourishes as my son dies
Corn, beans, tomatoes run rampant
Under the August sun
His once strong body withers under
Bombardment from disease, chemicals, radiation
Those burgeoning vegetables will end quickly
Consumed by insects, frost or me
His courage has engraved tablets of admiration
In his short life he had had time
To sow seeds of joy and creativity
And to harvest their fruits
Your spirit has perennial space among the stars—
Godspeed, Paul!

Wilderness trips and poetry may not be viable therapy for everyone. As Jeanne Boone suggests in her letter, coming to terms with grief for some seems nearly impossible, especially to very private people unwilling to burden others with their tears. She writes: "All my life I've been, or certainly tried to be, a positive person. . . . Through the years we've suffered many blows, we've had many problems and we've suffered other deaths, but losing our daughter is something I simply have not been able to accept. . . . I keep going because I know no other way. Besides, there are others of my loved ones who depend on me, who need me and who love me. However, those same loved ones have no idea how I really feel. Talking about our daughter's death is something I simply cannot do."

Yet, Jeanne had begun to do it. She started by writing a simple letter which turned into a floodgate opened. She also has read extensively: "Reading is the one thing that has helped me to some degree these past 18 months. I have read everything I can get hold of on life after death. If I didn't I'd never make it. I know our daughter has started a new life in a new world. I know she enjoys perfect health and she has happiness, contentment and peace. I know we will see her again when we get to go join her."

And she closes with this poem (of unknown source) sent to
her by her mother:

Life is eternal;
    and love is immortal;
and death is only a horizon;
    and a horizon is nothing
save the limit of our sight.

January 24, 1983

The Many Faces of Bereavement

Denial. Immobilization. Anger. Guilt. Depression.
These were the agonies most frequently expressed by readers who shared their personal bereavement experiences in
response to my January 24 column on the grief process.

LaVerne Skunberg, whose 24-year-old son died in an
accident six years ago, writes: "No matter how one handles
it, there will always be times when nothing helps. When the
'no help' [stage] happens to me, I am totally immobilized.
For a space in time I feel that if I move I will shatter.
Thankfully, the feeling soon passes and is overcome by the
raw pain of loss. I am better able to deal with the pain."

The discharge of anger frequently helps a grieving person
out of the helplessness and immobilization described by
Mrs. Skunberg. Some bereaved rage against the deceased
or against the circumstances which caused or surrounded
the death. Others direct their anger against the "pettiness"
of the everyday problems of associates when such "trivia" is
compared with the devastation of their own loss. One takes
out her fury on the sunshine: When a day dawns bright and
clear, she wants to "scream out that the sun has no right to
keep shining brightly as though nothing had happened."

Guilt accompanies anger in some cases, especially when
grief results from a death by suicide or the loss of a young
child. A Denver area woman writes: "It took several years

after [my son's suicide] to forgive myself: If I had done this . . . or maybe this . . . or this. . . . If only . . . if . . . if . . . if—STOP!"

Another respondent details the suicide of her 28-year-old brother: "Besides sorrow, my primary feeling since his death has been guilt. I have thought that I should have spent more time with him, should have called him more often when he was in emotional pain."

The parent of a 3-year-old who died after a short illness writes: "The most difficult part of coping with his death are the feelings of guilt. Quite often when my living child (age 5) gets sick, I relive the death, and my ministrations which were not quite right or enough to help my first child get well."

The "Why?" or the "Why me?" questions often dominate the grief process of those whose bereavement is the result of an accident or is otherwise premature. A 40-year-old minister whose wife was killed in a boating accident while saving their youngest child feels that it is only natural to scream "Why?"

"The soul's primary hunger is not for pleasure or for power, but rather for meaning," he writes 16 months after the tragedy. "It is meaning which makes our lives worth living and it is meaninglessness which moves the soul in the direction of death. . . . Somehow this field must be plowed so that some good fruit may be reproduced."

Yet, it usually will be months, even years, before "good fruit" will be recognized as resulting from the loss of a loved one. Mourners cannot be hurried through this process by well-meaning friends, but must be allowed to experience their loss, anger, guilt, and pain. The Reverend Stuart Haskins writes of a parishioner who said, "My neighbor tells me I should not grieve, because my husband is with God, but, God help me, I want him to be with me!"

After a period of months or years, when what psychologists call the "grief work" is done, most mourners experience what the Rev. Mr. Haskins terms "a return to hope and effective reality." Some are even able to "plow the field so some good fruit is produced."

A Denver widower who had considered suicide after losing his wife is finally able to write; "I reflect no longer on the 'Why me', 'What if', 'I should have' thoughts. Those thoughts are exterminators of the good life."

LaVerne Skunberg expresses her determination to keep going in the last stanza of a poem written at her son's grave:

The towering peaks wait silently, their hope to give
The pain wracked mind tries reaching out
For promise, seen but hardly understood,
Resigns itself, accepts as positive, the will to live.

A Denver mother tells of the spiritual growth she has attained in the painful years she spent coming to terms with both the death of her daughter in a car accident and the suicide of her son: "Life is a gift . . . even if children die before parents. Let me share with you . . . I'm overwhelmed. When I think that my two children could have come into this manifestation for my soul's growth . . . not theirs . . . mine . . . what love! I'm in awe, as I have grown spiritually and I say, humbly, 'Thank you, God.' "

Books recommended by readers: *When Bad Things Happen to Good People*, by Harold S. Kushner; *To Live Again*, by Catherine Marshall; *Death Be Not Proud*, by John Gunther; *To Live Until We Say Goodbye*, by Elisabeth Kubler-Ross and M. Warshaw; *If I Die and When I Do*, by Franki and Barbara Sternberg; *A Grief Observed*, by C.S. Lewis; and *The Bereaved Parent* by Harriet Schiff.

February 28, 1983

Coming to Terms with Bereavement

How do the bereaved work through the process of loss? How do people who have lost loved ones do what psychotherapists term the "grief work"? Readers responding to my January 24 column wrote openly and poignantly of their sorrow and what steps they took to come to terms with it.

A Denver widow whose husband died unexpectedly seven years ago writes: "First I wrote personal thank-you notes to each person who befriended me in any way at the time of his death . . . over 500 of them. My volunteer work took on a new dimension and I worked hard. . . . These projects helped me fill the lonely void in my life. In short, helping others in various ways has helped me to adjust emotionally to my husband's sudden death."

Hard work is mentioned by others as an antidote to grief. Yet some question its validity if taken to the extreme. "I don't disagree with the advice, 'keep busy,' but I think it should be given carefully. In my own situation I eventually realized I was becoming so physically exhausted, I was less able to cope with my emotional disarray," writes a woman who lost her grown son in an accident. "Coping with grief is a solitary thing. My personal journey has been a two-pronged effort. I wrote and played golf, both maniacally at times."

A woman whose 27-year-old son died of cancer emphasizes the importance of encapsulating the good times connected with the deceased. At the urging of a concerned friend she took a writing course and began to chronicle the happy and humorous events of her son's life. "As I would put the words down on paper, I could not think about anything else except what I was writing, and these were all good thoughts. It took hours, weeks and months to get the first article finished. I continued to write a few more short stories and all of this helped me through this painful period of my life."

Concentrating on positive memories gives solace to another grieving woman who lost her 17-year-old daughter in an automobile accident: "Would I have refused to have had Joy in my family, had I known she would die at 17 years of age? Think of all the fun times you've had—the laughter, the cuddling, the love, the funny times, the illness times, the school times, the friends. How much she gave to you in quality times. Would I have wished to have never known Joy? No! I would have wanted Joy for any length of time."

A woman who lost her 4-month-old baby to sudden infant death syndrome speaks of the difficulty of overcoming grief when there are so few memories. "What you are mourning is not memories but dreams. That is so terribly hard."

Some find the routine chores of putting the deceased's things to rest therapeutic: "[My sister and I] did not rush to empty mother's home and to distribute her possessions," writes Carol Stewart, who recently lost her 75-year-old mother. "We followed all her wishes which she had carefully and neatly written for us. We spent many days laughing and crying as we came across the items Mother had saved from our childhoods and we, in turn, repacked them and continued to save them."

Although "coping with grief is a solitary thing," friends, family, neighbors, and support groups are mentioned time and again: "I don't think it is possible to overemphasize that immediate and continuing action of caring by friends and neighbors," writes the woman who lost her grown son in an accident. "I treasured notes from friends and acquaintances who recalled warm and nurturing incidents with Mike— little things I had never known about. I heard many stories of his lending a helping hand, a kind word, a supporting action, and I hung these like medallions of reinforcement around my aching heart."

A Colorado Springs woman who lost her 37-year-old sister to a malignant brain tumor adds: "Hopefully the pain eases with time, but each life is so significant, no matter one's station in life, we all want to be reassured that the person we loved will never be forgotten."

Relations between family members of a survivor can be crucial. "I know that the only way I can assuage that guilt [over my brother's suicide] and make amends to my brother is by reaching out to the survivors," writes a young woman who also encloses a poem to her deceased brother and her remaining family. The concluding lines of the last stanza read:

> May your torn heart teach us all to mend ours,
> May this be our amends to you,
> And may our memories of you
> Be woven into that family fabric
> Tapestry of time.

For those who wish peer help in their grief process, the following resources may be listed in the telephone directory: Hospice, Grief Education Institute, The Compassionate Friends, SIDS (Sudden Infant Death Syndrome), Widowed Persons Service, and THEOS (They Help Each Other Spiritually).

March 7, 1983

Giving Help When Help Is Needed

A couple we knew was initiating a trial separation. Later, after they reconciled, the woman wrote to me in response to a message I had sent them during the time they were apart.

"You were so thoughtful to show you cared," she wrote. "It was a shame that many people were so threatened by 'another going-under' that they couldn't respond at all."

"Another going-under." Whether it's a marriage deteriorating, an illness that could prove fatal, or the death of someone else's loved one, how quick we are to distance ourselves from acquaintances' trauma.

If a couple is divorcing we may think: But that couple seems so much like us! We thought they had worked out their problems. Have we worked out ours? Fear. We should call, but which one do we contact? Him? Her? Both? Threatened and confused, we do nothing.

If an illness strikes, we are even quicker to dissociate. That business acquaintance who just had a heart attack. He seemed so healthy. As we push off the descending cloud of fear, what do we do for the heart attack patient? Often nothing.

Tragedy, or just plain difficulty, hits people we know; instead of responding, we wrap ourselves tightly in cloaks of denial. We act as if we see no evil, hear no evil, and ignore all evil, it won't happen to us. My friend's note reminded me how appropriately I responded this time; it also reminded me of the many other times I had not responded to acquaintances in distress.

Sometimes our denial is compounded by truly not knowing what to say. And, until we experience trauma ourselves, we haven't yet learned that the form of the message or the choice of words doesn't matter as much as the fact that we send them.

Readers who responded to my February series on grief wrote of how crucially important friends were to them in their mourning process. Some respondents gave advice to potential friends of others in grief or in trouble. A Colorado Springs woman who lost her 37-year-old sister to a brain tumor wrote: "The most important thing to do is *something* rather than nothing at all. Most people do not realize how desperately you need to hear from them, and it is never too late to respond. . . . Take the initiative to take food, send cards, or flowers, run errands, and care for children."

Other readers sent words of caution and advice which could best be summed up by the phrase, "Try to walk in the moccasins of the traumatized person before you speak." Do not tell a grieving person, particularly a grieving child, not to cry. A young woman writes, "My grandfather died in my home when I was 15. I went alone to sit and cry. My uncle, unfeeling, walked over to me and said I must not cry, to stop. . . . I decided then I would never tell someone not to cry. It is the most healing way to deal with grief."

Do not say, "It's for the best," even if in your opinion the demise of the deceased person was timely or ended suffering. If it is for the best, the grieving person will eventually see that, after he or she has had time to mourn. A person in grief must not be hurried.

If you have neglected to write that note, make that phone call, or send those flowers, and then unexpectedly meet up with an acquaintance in grief or illness, simply extend your condolences on the spot. Don't recount the reasons why you didn't respond earlier; a sufferer should not have to add your guilt to his or her burdens.

Do not falsely encourage the dying patient. "For the dying patient to *listen* in a non-judgmental manner is difficult at best, yet in a patient's case almost imperative," writes the woman who lost her sister. "Well-meaning suggestions of thinking positively, increased physical exercise, miracle healing, or ideas for 'getting well' may not enhance the patient's acceptance of their circumstances and impending death."

On the other hand, do not inadvertently discourage the recovering patient. At my first public appearance after my mastectomy in 1981, a well-meaning woman rushed up to me and said, "I'm so sorry about your surgery. I just had a friend die of breast cancer. Here is her husband's phone number, in case your husband needs it."

Yet, with a little tact and foresight, almost anything one says or does for a troubled friend will be taken kindly and appreciatively. A Denver woman who lost her son in an accident writes: "Friends don't have to be strong, just present, and willing to listen. One wonderful neighbor came immediately and said, 'At times like this I have the strength of warm Jello, so I just came to cry with you.' "

"Human beings are God's language," said Rabbi Harold S. Kushner, author of *When Bad Things Happen to Good People*, in a recent Denver address. Whether it is a marriage going under, a friend succumbing to a dread disease, or an associate grieving the loss of a loved one, let's not be afraid to speak.

April 25, 1983

X: Floodgates

For all those who have learned life might be shorter than they planned—

I'm not afraid of the storm for I can steer my own boat.
Louisa May Alcott

It was morning in the hospital two days after my modified radical mastectomy. The words which ebbed, flowed, and sometimes caught mid-air between my husband and me touched on our lives' goals, the kids' schedules, changes we would have to make. Sometimes we were heavily "into," other times we consciously avoided "the subject."

"Got to go," Dick said with a quick hug and kiss. "Remember the bat?" (The bat. I'd almost forgotten. The black-winged creature that descended down the chimney of the master bedroom to stalk and mystify us the night I found I would have to have a biopsy.) "I wrote you a poem. . . ."

The Night the Bat Came into Our Lives

Insidious black rodent
  You appeared unexpectedly
Casting a dark shadow
  Over our lives.

Unwelcome intruder
  Are you pest or pestilence?
Have you come to
  Malign or murder?

Were we too happy?
Did we insult the Gods?

Why—Pray why—Us—
Did we commit the sin of hubris?

Old, yet new
The eternal question arises
    Who? Why?
Is it by plan—
    Or Whim?

Are you gone, or
Do you linger still—
A biological medfly, to
Appear unexpectedly in the
    Richness of her body.

In these refined times
Our anesthetized musak society
Dulls and stills our rage.

We lack the volcanic human emotions
    The Rage of Lear
    The Passion of Dante
    The Sorrow of Juliet.

So
Let me say simply
That without you
    The days would be longer—the nights
                                    Eternity.

Easter would be empty
August—austere
Christmas—cruel.

You are the fire that
    Warms our lives
The sun around which
    Our family orbits.

We need you to
    Grace our retirement

To bless our grandchildren
To teach us all how to live and love.
                        We need you.
                        Get well—

                Richard D. Lamm, September 1981

                        * * *

   Traditionally the woman has been muse to the man, but
this time, no. My husband (who doesn't write poetry) wrote
a poem to me (who doesn't write poetry) and his muse, his
love, his tone, opened a floodgate of my own:

How I love my husband's muse
   The muse who watched Shakespeare
   The night we first met
   A Night without kisses
   Yet a night ripe with clues

To a man who would echo Richard III
   On a mountain ridge
   In winter's white wind:
   and Dickinson
   In the valley—where the wind's song
                        had dimmed.

Of late we have turned from his muse so dear
   though outsiders perceive it
   soft but clear.

He: Too challenged
      Too worried—too preoccupied
      Incensed by life's practical,
      Worrisome side.

I: Secretly jealous of the richness
      Of his bloom
      While tentatively searching
         for my own special flower

Speaking of other things—
Frightened of his muse's power.

Our children: Buoyed from room to room
                By the stereo's boom and blare
                Tin music erasing
                Their childlike awe
                Eroding each one's
                Individual flair.

(Have we all been stunted by the world's incessant roar?
If so—We must—we *will* be restored!)

My husband:
    His muse is his richness
    It is his Soul
    The vision which sets him above the other men
    Of tough body
    Other men
    Of strong goal.

His muse is his essence
    Neglected too long
    We have allowed it to hide
    Blasé to its song.

How I love my husband's muse
How I love my husband.

                                Rose Hospital, September 1981

* * *

But Today I Smile with Wonder

My breast is gone; I dare to look
Not feeling crucially marred,
I eye the smooth flat skin with wonder
Emotionally detached from the surgical scar.

The image arises of a mythical beast

Half woman, half ten-year-old child
Not so much loss and grief
Just an eerieness—strange, but mild.

"Why?" I joke to my Doctor
"Can't you make such smoothness of facial skin?"
"You can't have everything at once,"
he answers with a grin.

I know, I know
And perhaps that's what went wrong.
I thought I could, and
Working for perfection with too much hubris—
Sang only life's happy songs.

Yet just suppose one could have:
The skin of a babe
The breasts of a girl eighteen
The legs of an athlete twenty
The stature of a queen.
The wisdom of the ancient,
Yet the brain of twenty-one
The energy of twenty-five
When most sorrows
haven't begun.

Some do have it all
At least they seem to for a while
And reactions to their well-rounded excellence, from others
Is smile—after smile—after smile.

But such rewards can be
Empty, unfulfilling and not blest
Why? Perhaps
Until something is gone
We don't appreciate the rest.

I know I'm still in shock—
That I may "flip out" and yell,
By tomorrow

Damning the devil
For my piece of earthly hell.

I'll cry for the emerald
Bathing suit, stretchy, slinky and new
For the damnedest inconvenience
This illness puts everyone through.

Hysterical, bitter, unbearable
Such moods will come.
"The angry survive," I am told.

"Fine" I say—"Let it be."
I never have been much—
For rigid steely control.

Bitchy, ornery I may become
Through chemotherapy's strife
But today I smile with wonder
Thanking God for my life.

Rose Hospital, September 1981

* * *

A Day Among The Flowers

My husband sits reading among the flowers.
The hospital chair, his suit both blue
The morning sun dances through slit curtains
The autumn day begins fresh and new.

My heart leaps wildly from its bandage
I wake awash with joy. I absorb
His bearing—worldly, serious;
His skin yet like that of a boy.

A love of twenty years flows through my veins,
(Still reading—his expression stays serene)
A love purged of pettiness
Emerges—untarnished, brilliant, clean.

This scene will not linger—thank God!
Tomorrow the hospital will be far away.
Leaving this room, of course,
Is the goal, the triumph of the stay—

But as we return to harsher alarm clock wakeups
With our new found faith and power
May we discover some symbolic way
To begin each day "among the flowers."

Rose Hospital, September 1981

* * *

In mid-September I went home to my mother's house in
Palo Alto, California, to recuperate from the surgery. I was
warmed and nourished by her love, her cooking, and the
warm California sun; but my sleep was irregular, my dreams
disturbed:

Night Dreams at Home in Palo Alto

Sometimes it seems like bliss to die
   I see former boyfriends passing by—with sighs
   averting their grief
   from the eyes of their wives.

How simple and glorious—immortality
   People naming buildings after me
   The "Dorothy V. Lamm" Woman's Center
   The cornerstone lasts to eternity.

An anthology of my poems could raise
   The last needed money to pass the E.R.A.
   I'd be remembered with the famous feminists
   A few months? weeks? days?

My son freed from my nagging concern
   Protecting his private soul at every turn
   He'd cry, but he'd survive. Be closer to his father
   With kindling, their love would burn.

My daughter? Her heart would ache.
   But so wonderful my surrogates
   A Sister I love—
   Other sisters-in-law "en family"
   Closer to her in age and spirit
   Then perhaps her mom could be.

It seems so much cleaner to go
   from here straight to there
Easier than chemotherapy, nausea, and
   losing my hair
Than starting each day with medication and
   prayer—each minute a struggle
   not to go there.

I wake in a sweat—drenched with
   small beads throughout
I don't want to die! I need to reach out!
What scares me I say
   to my sister
   as she picks up the phone
Is that it wasn't frightening at all
It was like going home.
Am I giving up?
I'm not even "terminal"—but will
   passive dreams of death
   render my treatment nill?

Take it easy she says
   matching calm to my strife
There's days for everyone when death
   looks more glorious than life.
You're not giving up
You'd fight if you got near
Sometimes we must see death's tunnel
   To laugh at our illusions
   To remind us life is dear.

You could re-unite with Dad

drink tea on a cloud
Look down at us with detached love
    which demands nothing
    so pure—so proud.

How grand our visions of immortality
    But you won't cop out
    You're too ornery!

Palo Alto, September 1981

* * *

Other mini-vacations followed—all helping to restore my vigor. An ingrown and self-centered time; grandiosely I imagined nature itself reflecting my fears:

The Lake at the Broadmoor

How smooth the glistening surface of the lake
Hardly a ripple disturbs the air
I dip in my toes, but not too deep. . . .

Not probing beneath the unruffled surface
preserves our sanity, our "savoire faire."

Suppose we knew deep—the muddy waters
exactly what our lives held in store
Only if good—I want to know. I shudder

Save the evil for the murky future
Bury deep the "nevermores."

Colorado Springs, September 1981

* * *

But it was in Denver that I had my chemotherapy treatments; it was at home where I recovered slowly each day after the shots. The nausea and the hair loss were minimal, but the tiredness and depression for each 24-hour period after treatment were always debilitating and frequently overwhelming:

A Shadow of Myself

Suddenly I look like their grandmother
  Telescoped at mealtime from afar
    They are they—I am me—but I am
      older, shrivelled, marred.

My husband's robust sensuality
  is more than I can bear. My sexual
    center is a shadow of
      What—just when?—was there.

Just yesterday I was young, wife mother
  but when I'm ill from treatment
    I grow older. It's not the "minding"
      but the "not minding"
        that's the ultimate scare.

The gray-haired grandmother fades
  I see them with a woman—new—young.
    Behold a babe in arms! The tiny, snuggly
      infant—brings out my own
        children's charms.

The vision!
I should be wildly jealous—I should yell
  and scream . . . so soon! What ? You dare!
    Perhaps I'll yell tomorrow
      Today I'm too ill to care.

Ill from my cure. Relax. Stay non-delusional—
  Stay sound. Tomorrow that woman will be
    me again—body firm—hair light brown
      And I won't have to deal with envy—
        'Cause I'll be here forever.
          Maybe.

                    Denver, October 1981

* * *

Why?

Why Why Why
Not why me—but why I
I did it right—I deserve better—
Better than just "good try"

I watched and watched
I checked and checked
But they eluded me
Fearsome dark points on the screen

If I'd caught it three years earlier
My biopsy might have come clean

My publicity helped five women
"You saved my life!" they cry
Their lymph node involvement is minimal
They will surely not die.

No history in my family
No reason for yearly X rays—
The Doctor said—and I agreed.
Scared of excessive radiation,
I wouldn't have gone anyway.

No reason to go for X rays. No reason to have
this disease. No reason. . . .
Why Why Why
Not why me
Not why I
Just Why?

Denver, October 1981

* * *

The Medical Building

The woman sways unsteadily on her husband's arm
Her cheek is grossly swollen.

Tomorrow, unanesthetized, she will be sore
Feeling her jaw has been stolen.

A root canal—a wisdom tooth
   Various infections unknown?
   For a few days she will languish with pain
   Perhaps she'll moan and groan.

I enter the elevator unassisted. Walking straight, head
high—
   Dressed in heels, makeup intact—
   The glance of the delivery boy says:
   "Not bad looking, in fact."

But I envy the woman's swollen cheek.
   Feeling sick with revelation.
By this weekend she'll be free.
   Boring cocktail party guests
   with details of her operation.

The bitch! Why such appalling envy!
   I smile and let the "invalid" go first
   as the elevator opens at G.

She cannot see my pain
   It's of a different kind you see
   Her doctor's door said "Dentist"
   My door's "Oncology."

Denver, November 1981

* * *

Away again, removed from treatment sessions, I realized
that my attitude toward life had gone through numerous
cycles since the onset of my illness:

Equilibrium

Deep within I feel well again.
Oh, the cells could still be dividing
   But the bone scan is clear.

A long life seems possible—
  And since surgery
  Far more dear.
I don't know for sure—
  Of course
  One never will.
  Every fibre of my existence knows
This disease could get me still.
  But later, not sooner—so why fret.
Somewhere, somehow, sometime,
  Something will get me yet.
One breast traded
  For joy, peace, serenity,
  More time for jest, more space for rest.
An even bargain. I am pleased.
  But my thoughts make me sink to my knees.
Dare I bargain with God— ?
  Dear God, This is my fee—
  One breast will allow me eternity.
Not just me—but my family.
  Now that I've paid my price
I've become initiated to pain—
  I, who felt guilty, about having things so nice.
My daughter will blossom—resistant to fear and torment
My son will avoid the cruel bruises of a burly adolescence
My husband will prosper, produce and thrive.
Our whole family, God will keep healthy and alive
Because my breast is gone—all else will stay.
  Pleasant and mellow—
  Day after day.
I laugh rudely at my hubris, ashamed of the confidence
herein.
  I who know little theology,
  Know bargaining is a sin.
I mellow and know my getting sick or getting well
  Is no guarantee.
Things won't happen because of

Or instead of
Things that will be, will be.
But I still thank God for my illness—
    Strange to feel so blessed.
Just the new serenity of spirit—
    has been worth all the rest.

Arizona, November 1981

* * *

Five months later, our whole family took a scuba diving
vacation. There, I realized that my writing and poetry had
not centered on my illness since December. If I can move
away from it, I must be conquering it:

It's I!

Orion's belt is tight and bright
The stars twink messages through the night
My soul springs—upward
I rejoice in living
I love the fight.

There was a time I might have died
death sat on my shoulder
defied! defied!
Since then each day I rejoice in life
even when living is marred, maimed, or
scarred with strife.

I even love the barely pretty
the things one calls, the "nitty gritty"
Duties once resented in a subconscious way
Chores small and trivial that nagged at my day.

Making school lunches each morn
I still reel as I whiff the tuna, mayonnaise—
but I'm glad it's I—not a surrogate
with this motherly malaise.

I despise the stereo blaring intense;
but halleluliah!—It's I—It's I!!
Still enclosed within
its earthly, audio fence.

I hate sorting junk mail from the bills—
but it's my hands that do it
and as far as I can project the future
No one else's will.

Keeping track of the schedules of husband and each child
Drives me crazy, frustrated, and wild
Sewing costumes for skating shows or Halloween
not my favorite chore
hardly my dream.

But it's I, it's I, I and no other—
reaping both the rewards and tribulations of being their
mother!

How do I explain my new centeredness?
A love encompassing even jobs I hate?
It's that all living seems joyous
When the alternative could have been my fate.

                              Grand Cayman: April 1982

                    * * *

On October 20, 1982, I went for my last chemotherapy
treatment in my 13-month series:

The Last Treatment

Today I'm injected with my final shots
   And I don't know how I'm feeling
   Vile tubes—seven will empty into my veins
   for the thirtieth time
   their force sending me reeling.
   (The chemical taste rises in my throat.)

I will watch detached

Cytoxin is made of World War I mustard gas—
Strong enough to eradicate cancer
Did it?
Have I passed?
What other cells might it have killed?

"My wife is being poisoned twice a month,"
    said my husband last December
His countenance strained and chilled.
(Don't think that way—it's a cure.)

Impatience, not relief
    is my dominant mode
Anxious to be done
Irritable with the blood tests
    The weight tests
    The ice cap. Ugh.
Begone! All!
I want to hit the road!
(The sun is shining and the Fall leaves wait to be kicked.)

Yet chemotherapy has added
    a cradling structure to my life.
Has made me pace and rest
excused me from onerous jobs
with others understanding
that I should make each day my best.
(Secretly I've loved the pampering.)

It also has been a chemical crutch
    an assurance
    an atonement
    all this punishment
    must be making me well!
Has it?
They say four years will tell.
(I shiver in spite of the sunshine.)

Now that treatment is over
    I have only will power

meditation and prayer
And, oh yes
diet
vitamins
and daily exercise in fresh air.
(I feel so small.)

One friend became depressed
not joyous
over terminating her chemotherapy
"Help!" she said
"I'm alone, no medicine—
my cure now depends
only on God and me."
(She felt small too; I will call her.)

"How do you handle that 20 percent chance
you will have a recurrence?"
said the woman
last month
at a meeting.

"Daily and calmly," I answered
but my heart lurched
took precipitous skips
in its usually regular beating.

"Is it *really, really* your last treatment?"
asked my daughter
this morning
eyes gleaming—
over eggs and sizzling bacon.
When I said I was confident
but could not promise her
she looked let down, forsaken.

Will I live to see her children born
(Will I? Will I?)
is what she really wants to know
Oh, I think so

In fact I'm sure so
But to *promise* would be
  deceitful
  forced bravery
  delusional show

Relief. Impatience. Fear. Joy. Hope.
  Such undulating separate waves
  over me are stealing
  Today's my last chemotherapy
  I still don't know how I'm feeling.

Denver, October 1982

* * *

I'm Done!

At my desk
  The tears come sudden, hot and dry
  constricting throat bands loosen
  A sob of joy seems to come from behind me
  A strange, unnerving illusion.

Rushing out
  My Nikes scuffle with the crinkling leaves
  I jump and laugh and yell
  It's over! The hell. The hell. The hell.

Dizzy I roll down the slope, inhaling the October sun
  My green running suit picks up matching grass
  I feel at one with nature
  I'm done. I'm done. I'm done!

Denver, October 1982

Expanded Table of Contents